KIM
DAE-JUNG

KIM
DAE-JUNG

Norm Goldstein

CHELSEA HOUSE PUBLISHERS
PHILADELPHIA

Produced by Combined Publishing, Inc.

CHELSEA HOUSE PUBLISHERS

Editor in Chief: Stephen Reginald
Managing Editor: James Gallagher
Production Manager: Pamela Loos
Art Director: Sara Davis
Director of Photography: Judy L. Hasday
Senior Production Editor: Lisa Chippendale
Publishing Coordinator: James McAvoy
Cover Design and Digital Illustration: Keith Trego

The Chelsea House World Wide Web site address is
http://www.chelseahouse.com

1 3 5 7 9 8 6 4 2

Library of Congress Cataloging-in-Publication Data

Goldstein, Norm.
        Kim Dae-jung / Norm Goldstein.
            p.   cm. — (World leaders past and present)
        Includes bibliographical references and index.
        Summary: A biography of the man who survived imprisonment and
    attempts on his life during his efforts to bring democracy to South Korea
    and was elected President in 1997.
        ISBN 0-7910-5215-X (hc.)
        1. Kim, Dae Jung, 1925—Juvenile literature. 2. Presidents—Korea
    (South)—Biography—Juvenile literature. 3. Korea (South)—Politics
    and government—Juvenile literature. [1. Kim, Dae Jung, 1925-
    2. Presidents—Korea (South)]   I. Title. II. Series.
    World leaders past and present.
    DS922.42.k556G65   1998
    951.9504'3'092—dc21
    [B]   98-44316
                                                                      CIP
                                                                      AC

Contents

JOHN ADAMS
JOHN QUINCY ADAMS
KONRAD ADENAUER
ALEXANDER THE GREAT
SALVADOR ALLENDE
MARC ANTONY
CORAZON AQUINO
YASIR ARAFAT
KING ARTHUR
HAFEZ al-ASSAD
KEMAL ATATÜRK
ATTILA
CLEMENT ATTLEE
AUGUSTUS CAESAR
MENACHEM BEGIN
DAVID BEN-GURION
OTTO VON BISMARCK
LÉON BLUM
SIMON BOLÍVAR
CESARE BORGIA
WILLY BRANDT
LEONID BREZHNEV
JULIUS CAESAR
JOHN CALVIN
JIMMY CARTER
FIDEL CASTRO
CATHERINE THE GREAT
CHARLEMAGNE
CHIANG KAI-SHEK
WINSTON CHURCHILL
GEORGES CLEMENCEAU
CLEOPATRA
CONSTANTINE THE GREAT
HERNÁN CORTÉS
OLIVER CROMWELL
KIM DAE-JUNG
GEORGES-JACQUES
DANTON
JEFFERSON DAVIS
MOSHE DAYAN
CHARLES DE GAULLE
EAMON DE VALERA
EUGENE DEBS
DENG XIAOPING
BENJAMIN DISRAELI
ALEXANDER DUBČEK
FRANÇOIS & JEAN-CLAUDE
DUVALIER
DWIGHT EISENHOWER
ELEANOR OF AQUITAINE
ELIZABETH I
FAISAL
FERDINAND & ISABELLA

FRANCISCO FRANCO
BENJAMIN FRANKLIN
FREDERICK THE GREAT
INDIRA GANDHI
MOHANDAS GANDHI
GIUSEPPE GARIBALDI
AMIN & BASHIR GEMAYEL
GENGHIS KHAN
WILLIAM GLADSTONE
MIKHAIL GORBACHEV
ULYSSES S. GRANT
ERNESTO "CHE" GUEVARA
TENZIN GYATSO
ALEXANDER HAMILTON
DAG HAMMARSKJÖLD
HENRY VIII
HENRY OF NAVARRE
PAUL VON HINDENBURG
HIROHITO
ADOLF HITLER
HO CHI MINH
KING HUSSEIN
IVAN THE TERRIBLE
ANDREW JACKSON
JAMES I
WOJCIECH JARUZELSKI
THOMAS JEFFERSON
JOAN OF ARC
POPE JOHN XXIII
POPE JOHN PAUL II
LYNDON JOHNSON
BENITO JUÁREZ
JOHN KENNEDY
ROBERT KENNEDY
JOMO KENYATTA
AYATOLLAH KHOMEINI
NIKITA KHRUSHCHEV
KIM IL SUNG
MARTIN LUTHER KING, JR.
HENRY KISSINGER
KUBLAI KHAN
LAFAYETTE
ROBERT E. LEE
VLADIMIR LENIN
ABRAHAM LINCOLN
DAVID LLOYD GEORGE
LOUIS XIV
MARTIN LUTHER
JUDAS MACCABEUS
JAMES MADISON
NELSON & WINNIE MANDELA
MAO ZEDONG
FERDINAND MARCOS
GEORGE MARSHALL

MARY, QUEEN OF SCOTS
TOMÁŠ MASARYK
GOLDA MEIR
KLEMENS VON METTERNICH
JAMES MONROE
HOSNI MUBARAK
ROBERT MUGABE
BENITO MUSSOLINI
NAPOLÉON BONAPARTE
GAMAL ABDEL NASSER
JAWAHARLAL NEHRU
NERO
NICHOLAS II
RICHARD NIXON
KWAME NKRUMAH
DANIEL ORTEGA
MOHAMMED REZA PAHLAVI
THOMAS PAINE
CHARLES STUART PARNELL
PERICLES
JUAN PERÓN
PETER THE GREAT
POL POT
MUAMMAR EL-QADDAFI
RONALD REAGAN
CARDINAL RICHELIEU
MAXIMILIEN ROBESPIERRE
ELEANOR ROOSEVELT
FRANKLIN ROOSEVELT
THEODORE ROOSEVELT
ANWAR SADAT
HAILE SELASSIE
PRINCE SIHANOUK
JAN SMUTS
JOSEPH STALIN
SUKARNO
SUN YAT-SEN
TAMERLANE
MOTHER TERESA
MARGARET THATCHER
JOSIP BROZ TITO
TOUSSAINT L'OUVERTURE
LEON TROTSKY
PIERRE TRUDEAU
HARRY TRUMAN
QUEEN VICTORIA
LECH WALESA
GEORGE WASHINGTON
CHAIM WEIZMANN
WOODROW WILSON
XERXES
EMILIANO ZAPATA
ZHOU ENLAI

CHELSEA HOUSE PUBLISHERS

O N   L E A D E R S H I P

Arthur M. Schlesinger, jr.

LEADERSHIP, it may be said, is really what makes the world go round. Love no doubt smooths the passage; but love is a private transaction between consenting adults. Leadership is a public transaction with history. The idea of leadership affirms the capacity of individuals to move, inspire, and mobilize masses of people so that they act together in pursuit of an end. Sometimes leadership serves good purposes, sometimes bad; but whether the end is benign or evil, great leaders are those men and women who leave their personal stamp on history.

Now, the very concept of leadership implies the proposition that individuals can make a difference. This proposition has never been universally accepted. From classical times to the present day, eminent thinkers have regarded individuals as no more than the agents and pawns of larger forces, whether the gods and goddesses of the ancient world or, in the modern era, race, class, nation, the dialectic, the will of the people, the spirit of the times, history itself. Against such forces, the individual dwindles into insignificance.

So contends the thesis of historical determinism. Tolstoy's great novel *War and Peace* offers a famous statement of the case. Why, Tolstoy asks, did millions of men in the Napoleonic Wars, denying their human feelings and their common sense, move back and forth across Europe slaughtering their fellows? "The war," Tolstoy answered, "was bound to happen simply because it was bound to happen." All prior history predetermined it. As for leaders, they, Tolstoy said, "are but the labels that serve to give a name to an end and, like labels, they have the least possible connection with the event." The greater the leader, "the more conspicuous the inevitability and the predestination of every act he commits." The leader, said Tolstoy, is "the slave of history."

Determinism takes many forms. Marxism is the determinism of class. Nazism the determinism of race. But the idea of men and women as the slaves of history runs athwart the deepest human instincts. Rigid determinism abolishes the idea of human freedom—

the assumption of free choice that underlies every move we make, every word we speak, every thought we think. It abolishes the idea of human responsibility, since it is manifestly unfair to reward or punish people for actions that are by definition beyond their control. No one can live consistently by any deterministic creed. The Marxist states prove this themselves by their extreme susceptibility to the cult of leadership.

More than that, history refutes the idea that individuals make no difference. In December 1931 a British politician crossing Park Avenue in New York City between 76th and 77th Streets around 10:30 P.M. looked in the wrong direction and was knocked down by an automobile—a moment, he later recalled, of a man aghast, a world aglare: "I do not understand why I was not broken like an eggshell or squashed like a gooseberry." Fourteen months later an American politician, sitting in an open car in Miami, Florida, was fired on by an assassin; the man beside him was hit. Those who believe that individuals make no difference to history might well ponder whether the next two decades would have been the same had Mario Constasino's car killed Winston Churchill in 1931 and Giuseppe Zangara's bullet killed Franklin Roosevelt in 1933. Suppose, in addition, that Adolf Hitler had been killed in the street fighting during the Munich *Putsch* of 1923 and that Lenin had died of typhus during World War I. What would the 20th century be like now?

For better or for worse, individuals do make a difference. "The notion that a people can run itself and its affairs anonymously," wrote philosopher William James, "is now well known to be the silliest of absurdities. Mankind does nothing save through initiatives on the part of inventors, great or small, and imitation by the rest of us—these are the sole factors in human progress. Individuals of genius show the way, and set the patterns, which common people then adopt and follow."

Leadership, James suggests, means leadership in thought as well as in action. In the long run, leaders in thought may well make the greater difference to the world. But, as Woodrow Wilson once said, "Those only are leaders of men, in the general eye, who lead in action. . . . It is at their hands that new thought gets its translation into the crude language of deeds." Leaders in thought often invent in solitude and obscurity, leaving to later generations the tasks of imitation. Leaders in action—the leaders portrayed in this series—have to be effective in their own time.

And they cannot be effective by themselves. They must act in response to the rhythms of their age. Their genius must be adapted, in a phrase of William James's "to the receptivities of the moment." Leaders are useless without followers. "There goes the mob," said the French politician hearing a clamor in the streets. "I am their leader. I must follow them." Great leaders turn the inchoate emotions of the mob to purposes of their own. They seize on the opportunities of their time, the hopes, fears, frustrations, crises, potentialities. They succeed when events have prepared the way for them, when the community is awaiting to be aroused, when they can provide the clarifying and organizing ideas. Leadership ignites the circuit between the individual and the mass and thereby alters history.

It may alter history for better or for worse. Leaders have been responsible for the most extravagant follies and most monstrous crimes that have beset suffering humanity. They have also been vital in such gains as humanity has made in individual freedom, religious and racial tolerance, social justice, and respect for human rights.

There is no sure way to tell in advance who is going to lead for good and who for evil. But a glance at the gallery of men and women in *World Leaders—Past and Present* suggests some useful tests.

One test is this: Do they lead by force or by persuasion? By command or by consent? Through most of history leadership was exercised by the divine right of authority. The duty of followers was to defer and to obey. "Theirs is not to reason why / Theirs is but to do and die." On occasion, the so-called enlightened despots of the 18th century in Europe, absolutist leadership was animated by humane purposes. More often, absolutism nourished the passion for domination, land, gold, and conquest and resulted in tyranny.

The great revolution of modern times has been the revolution of equality. The idea that all people should be equal in their legal condition has undermined the old structure of authority, hierarchy, and deference. The revolution of equality has had two contrary effects on the nature of leadership. For equality, as Alexis de Tocqueville pointed out in his great study *Democracy in America*, might mean equality in servitude as well as equality in freedom.

"I know of only two methods of establishing equality in the political world," Tocqueville wrote. "Rights must be given to every citizen, or none at all to anyone . . . save one, who is the master of all." There was no middle ground "between the sovereignty of all and the absolute power of one man." In his astonishing prediction of 20th-century totalitarian dictatorship, Tocqueville explained how the revolution of equality could lead to the "*Führerprinzip*" and more terrible absolutism than the world had ever known.

But when rights are given to every citizen and the sovereignty of all is established, the problem of leadership takes a new form, becomes more exacting than ever before. It is easy to issue commands and enforce them by the rope and the stake, the concentration camp and the *gulag*. It is much harder to use argument and achievement to overcome opposition and win consent. The Founding Fathers of the United States understood the difficulty. They believed that history had given them the opportunity to decide, as Alexander Hamilton wrote in the first Federalist Paper, whether men are indeed capable of basing government on "reflection and choice, or whether they are forever destined to depend . . . on accident and force."

Government by reflection and choice called for a new style of leadership and a new quality of followership. It required leaders to be responsive to popular concerns, and it required followers to be active and informed participants in the process. Democracy does not eliminate emotion from politics; sometimes it fosters demagoguery; but it is confident that, as the greatest of democratic leaders put it, you cannot fool all of the people all of the time. It measures leadership by results and retires those who overreach or falter or fail.

It is true that in the long run despots are measured by results too. But they can postpone the day of judgment, sometimes indefinitely, and in the meantime they can do infinite harm. It is also true that democracy is no guarantee of virtue and intelligence in government, for the voice of the people is not necessarily the voice of God. But democracy, by assuring the right of opposition, offers built-in resistance to the evils inherent in absolutism. As the theologian Reinhold Niebuhr summed it up, "Man's capacity for justice makes democracy possible, but man's inclination to injustice makes democracy necessary."

A second test for leadership is the end for which power is sought. When leaders have their goal the supremacy of a master race or the promotion of totalitarian revolution or the acquisition and exploitation of colonies or the protection of greed and privilege or the preservation of personal power, it is likely that their leadership will do little to advance the cause of humanity. When their goal is the abolition of slavery, the liberation of women, the enlargement of opportunity for the poor and powerless, the extension of equal rights to racial minorities, the defense of the freedoms of expression and opposition, it is likely that their leadership will increase the sum of human liberty and welfare.

Leaders have done great harm to the world. They have also conferred great benefits. You will find both sorts in this series. Even "good" leaders must be regarded with a certain wariness. Leaders are not demigods; they put on their trousers one leg after another just like ordinary mortals. No leader is infallible, and every leader needs to be reminded of this at regular intervals. Irreverence irritates leaders but is their salvation. Unquestioning submission corrupts leaders and demeans followers. Making a cult of a leader is always a mistake. Fortunately hero worship generates its own antidote. "Every hero," said Emerson, "becomes a bore at last."

The signal benefit the great leaders confer is to embolden the rest of us to live according to our own best selves, to be active, insistent, and resolute in affirming our own sense of things. For great leaders attest to the reality of human freedom against the supposed inevitabilities of history. And they attest to the wisdom and power that may lie within the most unlikely of us, which is why Abraham Lincoln remains the supreme example of great leadership. A great leader, said Emerson, exhibits new possibilities to all humanity. "We feed on genius. . . . Great men exist that there may be greater men."

Great leaders, in short, justify themselves by emancipating and empowering their followers. So humanity struggles to master its destiny, remembering with Alexis de Tocqueville: "It is true that around every man a fatal circle is traced beyond which he cannot pass; but within the wide verge of that circle he is powerful and free; as it is with man, so with communities."

1

Sweet Victory

South Koreans danced in the streets.

In Seoul especially, tens of thousands spilled onto the thoroughfares to celebrate the election of a former dissident, Kim Dae-jung, as President of the Republic of Korea. Supporters surrounded his home on the outskirts of Seoul, dancing, cheering his name and popping open champagne bottles.

The mood was the most euphoric in Kwangju, in the southwestern region of Korea, where sixty thousand citizens gathered at the central plaza.

"Hurray! Hurray!" they shouted over and over again.

"Hurray! Hurray! Hurray!"

It was in Kwangju where government paratroopers had gunned down hundreds of pro-democracy protesters in 1980. The government had blamed Kim for fomenting that trouble. It had charged him with treason and had sentenced him to death. But Kim showed the resiliency that marked his political life. Under pressure from the United States, the government had commuted his

> *Throughout my life I have faced death five times. For six years I was in prisons, and for 10 years I was in exile or under house arrest. I never lost hope that someday there would be something like this.*
> —KIM DAE-JUNG
> Speaking about his election as President of South Korea

Kim Dae-jung waves to the crowd as he arrives for his inauguration ceremony, where he was sworn in as President of South Korea.

Supporters of Kim Dae-jung celebrate his election as President of South Korea. The veteran opposition leader, persecuted and imprisoned by military dictators, now faces the daunting job of restoring the nation's shattered economy.

sentence to twenty years and allowed him to go into self-exile.

For four decades, Kim had been the opposition leader. As the democratic dissident, he was in prison or under house arrest for more than seven of those years; in exile for another four. There were several attempted assassinations.

Kim had been Korea's chief champion of democracy, a beacon for students and workers who protested the dictatorship and finally forced it to bow to its first truly democratic elections in 1987.

On December 18, 1997, Kim Dae-jung, at the age of 72, after three unsuccessful attempts to rule his nation, became President of the Republic of Korea. The opposition had become the leadership. It was the crowning achievement of a maverick political career, culminating in the toppling of an establishment disgraced by scandal and economic crisis.

Victory was indeed sweet for Kim and his supporters.

Kim, of the opposition National Congress for New Politics, won 40.3 percent of the vote—with 10 million votes—beating Lee Hoi-chang of the ruling Grand National Party with 38.7 percent of the vote. Third was Rhee In-je of the New Party by the People. It marked the first change of power to another party since Korea began holding elections in 1948—the first time in the fifty years since the peninsula was split into separate nations, North and South, that the South Korean people had elected an opposition figure as President.

It was a relatively narrow victory and enthusiasm was somewhat tempered by the political and economic obstacles he faced.

But his election was truly astonishing; some compare it to that of Nelson Mandela's election in South Africa. Each was considered a danger to the ruling establishment; each was jailed for years and faced death sentences—and each persevered to become his nation's leader.

When Kim won his party's presidential nomination in the summer of 1997, Mandela sent him an old wristwatch with a faded, cracked leather band. It was the watch the anti-apartheid leader had worn through much of his turbulent political career, including his twenty-seven years in prison. Mandela said he hoped the watch would bring Kim luck. The watch now sits in Kim's office at the presidential Blue House, where he looks at it every day.

A telling insight into the character of Kim and his strong sense of justice was apparent in his first act as President-elect. He asked incumbent President Kim Young-sam—himself a former dissident—to grant amnesty to former presidents Roh Tae-woo and Chun Doo-hwan and release them from jail. This was the same Chun who had

Kim is respected as the beacon for democratization because he has led an indomitable life without yielding to suppression.
—KIM YOUNG-SAM
1987

15

Kim Dae-jung talks with out-going President Kim Young-sam during a meeting at the presidential palace just days after the December 1997 election. The two discussed amnesty for two ex-presidents, Chun Doo-hwan and Roh Tae-woo, who were jailed on charges including bribery and corruption.

sentenced Kim to death claiming he was a traitor in 1980.

The day after his victory, Kim spoke with U.S. President Bill Clinton, who extended his congratulations for what he called Korea's impressive exercise in democracy. Kim has had a long involvement with the United States where he lived for several years while in exile in the 1970s and 1980s and spent time at Harvard University. More importantly, the United States government intervened twice to save his life when it was threatened by authoritarian regimes in 1973 and 1980.

Just months after his election, he made a state visit to the United States, a personal and diplomatic triumph.

At home, the liberal newspaper *Hankyoreh Shinmun* editorialized:

> President Kim's efforts to pursue practical diplomacy were impressive. He was welcomed as a 'homecoming hero' who triumphed over a difficult situation during his struggle for democracy.... President Kim has consolidated the foundation for the relationship between Korea and the U.S. while groping to establish a new rela-

tionship between North and South Korea....

Moreover, the President produced results that will allow Korea to get over the current foreign currency debacle. These achievements should be praised.

Who is this "man of the masses," this "Asian Mandela"?

How was he able not only to survive imprisonments and attempts on his life, but persevere in his ideals and, eventually, conquer?

And could he lead his nation out of its economic mire and at the same time improve its complex foreign relations, especially with rival neighbor North Korea?

> *I have prepared myself for a long time for the job that I am about to undertake, and I am confident that I will do the best job that I am capable of doing....*
> —KIM DAE-JUNG
> In his inaugural address

2

Young Man with Dreams

Kim Dae-jung was born December 3, 1925, in Hugwang, a village on Ha-ui Island in the Cholla province. In Korean, a person's first name comes after his last name. Kim's first name, Dae-jung, means *the masses* or *the common people* in Korean. In later years, he was to use Hugwang, the name of his village, as a pseudonym sometimes.

Korea is a mostly mountainous East Asian peninsula between the Yellow Sea to the west and the East Sea to the east. Ha-ui is an isolated island off its southwest coast, surrounded by the Yellow Sea separating Korea from China. Indeed, the sea routes around the island were used for hundreds of years as gateways to China. Because of its warm sea currents, farmers on Ha-ui Island enjoy good crops of barley and rice and its inlets are a source of many varieties of shellfish. Some have referred to this serene and scenic island, dotted with bamboo and pine trees, as the hidden paradise.

> *My hometown Mokpo! I love Mokpo and I long for Mokpo. But, there are two contradictory faces to past and contemporary Mokpo. One side of it embodies sentiment and tears, while the other side embodies vitality in the pursuit of justice and development.*
> —KIM DAE-JUNG
> Speaking about his hometown

A young Kim, in a photo taken in 1943 when he was a student at the Mokpo Commercial High School. It was Mokpo, in southwestern South Korea, that later became the base of his political support.

It was in this tranquil atmosphere that Kim Dae-jung was brought into the world.

He was the second son of Kim Yun-shik, an upper middle class farmer whom Kim credits for his artistic talents, and Chang Su-kum, a strict but loving mother whom he says instilled in him a strong sense of right and wrong. He had two younger brothers, Dae-yee and Dae-hyun.

At the time of Kim's birth, and for fifteen years before, Korea was under the rule of Japanese imperial rulers, who made many of Korea's farmers hapless sharecroppers. In the previous century, neighboring Japan had forced Korea—which had been known as the "Hermit Kingdom" because it had closed itself off to outside contact—into diplomatic relations. In 1876, after a show of force by the Japanese navy, the two countries agreed to a commercial treaty that opened up three Korean ports, Pusan, Wonsan and Inchon, for Japanese trade and provided for an exchange of diplomatic missions. The agreement, called the Kanghwa Treaty, also gave extraterritorial rights to the Japanese in Korea and gave Japanese diplomats freedom of travel. Still, the Western powers of Great Britain and the United States, as well as China, were predominant in Korea—until about 1894. In that year the Chinese-Japanese rivalry broke into all-out war and Japanese troops moved into Korea. Japan's naval supremacy proved the decisive factor in this dispute and China sued for peace—giving up all claims to Korea.

Though technically now independent, Korea had to endure another neighborhood rivalry, this one between Japan and Russia. The powerful and militaristic Japanese were victorious again in this Russo-Japanese war of 1905 and imposed the Protectorate Treaty on Korea, taking over its foreign and financial affairs, its communications systems, and its police and military. The Japanese then extended their control to Korea's external affairs in a treaty signed on November 17, 1905.

Many former colonies of England and France have entered into amicable relations with their former rulers. If we refuse to establish diplomatic relations with Japan, even though we are equal with Japan, we are heading against the common trend of the world.
—KIM DAE-JUNG
speaking about plans to normalize relations with Japan in 1963

Every citizen had been harboring deep inside a desire to see him, and it is exploding out all at once.
—a white collar worker from Kim's home province of Kwangju during his visit there in 1987.

Thousands of people packed the streets in Kwangju to greet Kim Dae-jung on a 1987 visit to his native province. It was the first time Kim had been back to back the province where he was born, began his political career, and had received large support over the years.

Kim is in the second row, third from right, in this photo taken with his classmates at Mokpo Commercial High School.

By the time Emperor Sunjong ascended to the Korean throne in 1907, chosen by the Japanese to succeed Kojong, who was deposed for his part in an anti-Japanese uprising that year, the Korean government was almost completely in the hands of Japan. Then in 1910, Japanese rule was made official with a formal and forcible annexation, ending the centuries-old rule of the Choson dynasty of Korea, which had come into power in 1392.

Koreans deeply desired independence and demonstrated and worked to achieve that goal.

There were even assassination attempts—but nothing came of it until World War II and the defeat of Japan by Allied forces.

Because of this, Kim Dae-jung grew up among the Japanese in an occupied country.

In 1933, at the age of eight, Kim was sent to a new and modern grade school on Ha-ui Island, where he was admitted to second grade. When he was in the fourth grade, he was sent to Mokpo to transfer to Mokpo Primary School. Mokpo was to become his second home. The seaport on the southwestern coast was at the time a center for coastal marine transportation as well as a thriving shipping port for rice and cotton.

Kim seldom dwelled on the past, but while in prison years later, he told his grandchildren about his early years, beginning with what he described as a "difficult delivery" for his mother. "They say I was unconscious when I was born," he wrote. "In a village where there were no doctors or midwives, it was miraculous that I held onto life."

He recalled being fond of animals, to the point that he "wailed and caused quite a commotion" when villagers slaughtered and ate a dog that had been raised at home. He remembered his father carving a boat for him: "I still vividly remember him taking off his overcoat and making it." His memories of his father were that he was a very kind man, good at traditional singing and dancing. He wrote:

> When I was little my best playmate was my brother Dae-yee, who was two years younger. There was a big age difference with Dae-hyun, who was incredibly handsome when he was young. I tended to be well-behaved and rarely argued with others....
>
> I think it was about when I was about five years old that a rice-jelly peddler came to the village with rice-jellies and a variety of other items. He was in a drunken stupor, lying on the road. Older children began to steal his things, and they gave me a pipe that I took home to give to father. I remember being scolded by mother and going to the peddler with her to return it.

He reminisced about his early school days, remembering that he was admitted to the second grade at a four-year school that had been established for the first time on the island:

The admission at the time, was a turning point in my life. If I had not been admitted then, I would have been stuck in the countryside and buried there.

My dreamy and happy childhood took on a wholly new character when I was transferred to Mokpo when I was in the fourth grade. Memory of home makes anyone nostalgic, and for me, Hugwang village in a corner of a small, almost unknown island called Ha-ui is the birthplace I remember. Whenever I think about it, I cannot be

In 1974 at a special prayer session at a Catholic church in Seoul, Kim Dae-jung sits with his head bowed in prayer. Kim Dae-jung was raised to be a devout Catholic.

overcome with yearning and remembrances. You know very well that it is the reason for my pen name, Hugwang.

In 1937, Kim transferred to a six-year grade school, Pukkyo Primary School, where he excelled in all subjects and finished at the head of his class. He went on to be accepted at the Mokpo Commercial High School, no easy feat, since the Japanese colonial administration often restricted educational opportunities for Koreans. But Kim did quite well there, always at the top or second in his class. He was elected class representative, even though most of his classmates were Japanese. But, when he wrote a class essay decrying the Japanese rule, he was removed as class captain, branded by the Japanese teachers as holding "dangerous ideological tendencies."

After graduation in 1943, Kim was accepted at Manchuria University but, to avoid military conscription under the Japanese colonial rule, he went instead to work in the accounting and finance department of the Mokpo Marine Transportation Company.

With the end of World War II, the U.S. military command required the Japanese to dispose of the businesses and properties they owned in South Korea and Kim worked successfully to take over the company. He reorganized it, renamed it the Heung-Guk Marine Transportation Company, and became its president. The marine transportation business was booming at the time and Kim, still in his twenties, prospered as a businessman.

Like many Korean youths after the war, Kim sought out some political attachment. Communism was one ideology he looked into, but he was quickly disappointed in the experience. He was to write later:

Frankly speaking, I did not know clearly at that time as to what was communism or what was nationalism. Up to 1946, I participated in the meetings of the so-called

People's Committee or New Democratic Party, which were under the influence of the leftist front. In a short span of time, I joined various groups and repeatedly experienced, first, expectations and then, disappointments. Eventually, I met with communists and at one time, I was deeply curious about communism. I studied with deep concern as to whether communism could be a useful doctrine which could bring forth independence and happiness to our people.

Finally, I cut off all ties with communism. I had no other alternative but to cut off ties since I considered national independence as our supreme goal, while the communists with whom I was in touch at the time put higher priority on loyalty to the Soviet Union than on our national independence.

Kim had always been interested in the news and journalism. He had been a very good student, especially in history, and as a youth, had paid a good deal of attention to current affairs, "to the extent that I checked the front page of the newspaper each day," he once wrote. So when an offer came to take over the local *Mokpo Daily News,* which had been started by a Japanese company, he eagerly accepted it. He served as its publisher from 1946 through 1948.

On April 9, 1946, Kim married Cha Yong-ae, the oldest daughter of a distinguished community leader and one-time officer of the Mokpo chapter of the Korea Democratic Party, a key conservative political force in the country. Cha was well educated and a dedicated wife. The pair were to have two sons, Hong-il and Hong-up.

It was a happy and relatively prosperous time. Until June 25, 1950.

3

Invasion and Incarceration

When Japan's defeat in World War II was imminent, the United States proposed a plan that would separate the Japanese possession of Korea roughly in half, with the dividing line at the 38th parallel—a lasting division, as it turned out. At the time, however, after the surrender of Japan it was to be an administrative demarcation with two zones of Allied occupation. The South was to be under the Americans with their Soviet ally taking the northern half.

But, the Soviets saw the separation as something far different. They eventually cut rail lines and restricted movements of people and goods across the unnatural boundary.

In 1947, the United Nations scheduled elections in both halves of the country to determine the government of a unified Korea. On August 15, 1948, an election in the south resulted in the creation of the Republic of Korea, with Syngman Rhee as its first president.

Rhee's nationalist views had earned him a jail

Kim Dae-jung addresses a crowd of supporters denouncing the mismanagement and policies of the ruling party.

sentence as a young man, during which time he had been tortured. He had studied at United States universities, earning a Ph.D. from Princeton University in 1910—the year Japan annexed Korea. He had returned home, but was forced to flee and was a political exile in the United States until 1945, all the while remaining a vocal leader of Korea's independence movement, organizing a government-in-exile. He had been returned to Korea after the war by U.S. forces.

The Soviets, on the other hand, resisted any U.N.-sponsored elections and instead installed Kim Il Sung as premier of a communist regime.

As a youth, Kim Il Sung and his family had fled to Manchuria in 1925 to escape Japanese rule. He had joined the Korean Communist Party and fought the Japanese as a guerrilla leader. He had received military and political training in the then-Soviet Union and joined the Soviet army, serving as an officer during World War II. Under Soviet occupation, he established a communist provisional government and became premier when the Democratic People's Republic of Korea (North Korea) was established in 1948.

Post-World War II Korea had become two Koreas, each going separate ways, politically, ideologically and economically. They even wrote their names differently. North Korean names are generally three separate words, each starting with a capital letter; South Koreans usually hyphenate the second two names and use a lowercase letter after the hyphen. Both use the family name first.

Each, however, declared their intentions to unify the country—by force, if necessary. But North Korea's army was twice as large as South Korea's, and better equipped and trained. By 1950, North Korean patrols were regularly crossing the man-made border between the two Koreas; they eventually had nine military divisions deployed along the boundary.

At 4 A.M. on a rainy Sunday, June 25, 1950, North Korea's artillery fired across the 38th parallel before mounting a full-scale invasion by seven assault divisions of infantry supported by Soviet-made tanks.

Kim Dae-jung was on a business trip in Seoul that day. He was among the hundreds of thousands who were trapped in the city, which fell into the hands of the communists on June 28. Kim saw summary executions in the streets and worried, too, that he would be "recruited" by the communists for the "volunteer corps."

He and five others hired a boat, crossed the Han River and started the long march back to Mokpo. They narrowly escaped bombing attacks by the North Koreans and strafing flights from the U.S.-United Nations forces. It took them twenty days to reach Mokpo on foot.

Upon arrival, Kim found his house and its belongings taken over by the communists, and learned that his second son, Hong-up, had been born in an air-raid shelter on July 29 and his younger brother, Dae-yee, had been arrested. Three days later, Kim was himself arrested, guilty, apparently, only of being a successful businessman. He was imprisoned for the first time, and later recalled:

> *Politics should not be manipulated at will by dictators to suit their own needs.*
> —KIM DAE-JUNG

...My imprisonment under the Communists was unparalleled in its complete insulation from contact with the outside. Not only was any communication with the outside impossible, but there also was no freedom within the prison cell, such as freedom to converse with others or the freedom to make small bodily motions.

Kim was to be executed along with all the other inmates. They were taken out twenty at a time, to be executed by firing squad. When just eighty were left, including Kim, good fortune came their way. United Nations forces were attempting to recapture Seoul after a bold and risky amphibious landing on September 15, 1950, at Inchon, a major Korean port one hundred and sixty-five

Republic of Korea soldiers march toward the frontline in August, 1950, during Pusan perimeter battles.

miles behind the communist lines. At about the same time, U.N. troops were able to break out of the Pusan perimeter in the southeastern corner of South Korea—the only area not overrun by the North Koreans in their initial attacks. The war was now turning against the North Koreans and the prison guards had been ordered to withdraw immediately. The eighty remaining inmates, about to be executed, were brought back to the prison by local communist guards. There, they were able to kick down their cell door and escape.

It was the first of several narrow escapes from death for Kim. Others, though had not been as fortunate. Of the nine inmates in Kim's cell, six were executed. Kim's father-in-law was shot, but survived. Thousands of other civilians were branded as reactionaries and killed by the communists en masse. A few days later, Mokpo was liberated by South Korean and American forces.

Order was restored in many parts of South Korea, and Kim went back to the marine transportation business. In May 1951, he was named president of the Mokpo Merchant Ship Co. and chairman of the Mokpo chapter of the Korea Marine Transportation Association. He became quite well known in the community as both a successful businessman and journalist, as head of the *Mokpo Daily News.*

Still, the war continued. The North Koreans had been driven back over the 38th parallel and almost all the way to the Korean-Chinese border, when the newly established People's Republic of China sent hundreds of thousands of Communist troops to help the flagging North Korean army. This started a new phase of the war. U.N. troops were forced back, with much of the heaviest fighting of the war taking place that winter of 1950 in the cold northern mountain regions. By the spring, the fighting had produced a bloody stalemate—at roughly the same 38th parallel where it began. An armistice ending military hostilities wasn't signed until July 27, 1953. It provided for a cease-fire line which became a border between North and South, with a Demilitarized Zone separating the two countries. President Syngman Rhee would not sign the armistice. The two Koreas remain technically at war, having signed no treaty. Today, their border is the world's most heavily guarded, with two million troops still deployed on both sides.

The Korean War had been a war of prevention; it stopped the North Korean communist regime from conquering the South. Otherwise, it changed little; Korea still remained divided—physically, politically, and ideologically.

In 1954, at the age of twenty-nine, Kim expressed dissatisfaction with the regime of Sygman Rhee and felt confident enough to run for the National Assembly, or parliament, as an independent candidate from Mokpo, saying, "I have come to the conclusion that the real well-being of the people could not be attained unless a genuine democratic political system is firmly established by ending the dictatorship which ignores the will of the people and downgrades the National Assembly." With the support of organized labor through the Port Labor Union, the Korean Youth League, and journalists, he seemed a sure winner. But he lost to the government's Liberal Party which had mobilized all its political power to take the election.

In May 1956, Syngman Rhee was again a candidate for president. He had been elected by the National Assembly in 1948, and by popular vote in 1952—after a martial law proclamation in which many opposition leaders were jailed and the law changed to allow for popular election, two acts that made his re-election a certainty. Now, he had pushed a constitutional amendment through the National Assembly allowing unlimited terms for the president. The leading opposition party, the Democratic Party, nominated Shin Ik-hee to oppose him, with Chang Myon as the vice-presidential candidate. Kim supported Shin, but the candidate died suddenly just ten days before the voting. Rhee won the election, with Chang—from the opposition party—as vice president. In the fall of 1957, there was an assassination attempt on Chang. That incident led Kim to join the Democratic Party, choosing to fight the system rather than go along with the party in power.

Kim lost a parliamentary election in Inn-Jae District in 1958, but sued on the grounds of illicit election practices. The Supreme Court ruled in his favor and called for a supplementary election, in June 1959. The government's Liberal Party, however, prohibited its soldiers from attending campaign rallies or reading campaign leaflets and warned them not to vote for the opposition. In a district where the majority of eligible voters were soldiers who tended to vote for the opposition, this made a huge difference. Kim lost the election—and a good deal of money campaigning for it.

The ruling Liberal Party, aware of Kim's financial condition, made him a tempting offer, which Kim was to later recall:

While I was living in such a destitute condition, the Liberal Party tempted me many times to switch my party affiliation with an offer of a huge sum of money. Between 1950 and 1960, many opposition members could not stand the strain of poverty and many assemblymen switched their party affiliations.... But I overcame the temptations and carried on my struggle as my conscience dictated. It goes with-

Kim Dae-jung addressing the National Assembly in 1963. He first ran for a seat in the Assembly in 1954.

out saying that I owe my steadfastness to the encouragement and support rendered to me by my friends. But, I owe my greatest debt of gratitude to my deceased wife for her dedication.

Cha Yong-ae had died on May 29, 1960, after a long illness aggravated by the strains and pressures produced by the 1959 election defeat. Kim was to write in *Conscience in Action:*

Kim ran three times for the National Assembly. The third time, in 1961, he finally won the seat he desired but fate would take an unforeseen turn and he was never sworn in.

She never complained even a bit under the most painful circumstances, and inspired me with her courage. She used to encourage me by saying that 'you have to lead a life which won't be regretted, since

you are a man.' She used to tell me that 'even if you are arrested, don't worry about our household matters. Please fight like a man should do.' Her voice still rings clearly in my ears.

Kim remained dedicated to politics and his party.

During the 1960 election campaign, President Rhee's dwindling popularity was evident. There were charges of fraud and corruption in the government and general dissatisfaction with the economy. Students demonstrated against him in February, March, and April and university professors soon joined them. The Student Revolution of April 19 forced President Syngman Rhee to resign on April 26. He left for self-exile in Hawaii, where he died nine years later.

After four months of an interim government led by Ho Chong, Yun Po-sun was elected president. A new parliamentary-style constitution now gave greater political power to the legislature though the real political power was wielded by the prime minister, Chang Myon. At the end of July 1960, Kim decided to once again seek a seat on the National Assembly. He was a Democratic Party candidate for the Inn-Jae district. He lost, by less than one thousand votes, in an election that served to demonstrate his future potential. The winner ended up being disqualified for illegal past activity.

When a supplementary election was set in May 1961, Kim ran again as a candidate for the Democratic Party. Finally, he was declared the winner on May 14.

But it was not to be. The reason this time, and several times to come, was Park Chung-hee.

Park led a bloodless coup on May 16, 1961, that deposed the democratic, but politically unstable government, and dissolved the National Assembly to which Kim had been democratically elected.

Kim was never even sworn in.

> *You have to lead a life which won't be regretted, since you are a man. Even if you are arrested, don't worry about our household matters. Please fight like a man should do.*
> —CHA YONG-AE
> first wife of Kim Dae-jung

4

Sowing and Reaping a Political Career

Park Chung-hee had been educated at a Japanese military academy as a youth and served in the Japanese army in World War II. After the war, he switched to the South Korean army and rose to the rank of major general. Like many other Koreans at the time, he worried about the country's deteriorating economy and its political situation. He chose a non-democratic way to change it.

On May 16, 1961, at the age of forty-four, he led a group of other officers, including Lieutenant General Chang Do-yung, in a *coup d'etat*, forcing the resignation of President Yun Po-sun, establishing a military government and declaring martial law. All functions of government were taken over by the Supreme Council for National Reconstruction—headed by General Park, who was to be the dominant personality in South Korea for the next eighteen years. The coup apparently had been supported by most of the South Korean military and reportedly planned even before the student revolution that toppled Syngman Rhee. They had waited only to see what would happen under the interim Chang regime before acting.

A truly new era shall dawn from now on. A new epoch shall be marked for our party as well as for Korean politics. I shall fight for the freedom and well-being of our people as a vanguard of this new era.
—KIM DAE-JUNG
In his acceptance speech when made a presidential candidate in 1970

During his political career Kim faced many obstacles fighting for a democratic South Korea.

Park's Supreme Council, the chief organ of the military, took sweeping powers of detention and censorship. It also announced that power would be handed over to an elected civilian administration and the soldiers would be sent back to their barracks after his administration was set up and reforms accomplished. Instead, the military became more powerful. They were abetted by the establishment of the secret Korean Central Intelligence Agency (KCIA), headed by Kim Jong-pil, which helped crush all political opposition.

The military coup that installed Park Chung-hee as president of South Korea was the beginning of numerous confrontations between these two political enemies—and the start of Kim Dae-jung's dramatic rise as an opposition leader.

To begin with, the dissolution of the National Assembly by Park meant that Kim's election was voided. Then, just days after the coup, Kim was arrested by the military government; it was not to be the last time he was imprisoned by the Park regime. However, this time there were no specific charges against him and he was soon released. But, the next government move against him was worse. In March 1962 he was barred from taking part in any political activities for seven years, solely because he was a former member of the National Assembly, even if only for four days. Kim was among thousands who were thus deprived of speaking out politically by an authoritarian decree that wasn't lifted until early 1963.

Kim married for the second time on May 10, 1962. Lee Hee-ho was working at that time as the general secretary of the Korean Young Women's Christian Association (YWCA).

Lee was born September 21, 1922, in Seoul, a daughter in the line of the Lees of Chunju, the royal family of the last dynasty in Korea. She was the eldest girl of eight children; three brothers were older and a sister and three other brothers were born after her. Her father, Lee Yong-ki, was a physician.

She had attended Ewha Girl's High School and

Ewha Women's College, but World War II interrupted that education. After the war, she returned to school for a teaching certificate, then entered the Teacher's College of Seoul National University. Her education again was interrupted by war, the Korean War. She continued to study, this time in the United States, earning a masters degree in sociology at Scarritt College in Nashville, Tennessee.

Returning home in 1958, she taught at Ewha Women's University and worked as the executive director of the National YWCA in Korea. It was then that she had a chance encounter with Kim, "a young political aspirant with dreams and

Kim Dae-jung married Lee Hee-ho on May 10, 1962, after the death of his first wife.

hopes but with no future," she was to write later. "There was tremendous opposition from my family as well as among my friends to the very thought of my marriage to him. Despite all that, I felt greatly drawn to him. He was an avid and voracious reader even then. He used most of his available moments for acquiring knowledge through books. He treasured knowledge not merely as ideas or abstract concepts, but exhibited impressive will and sincerity to translate his knowledge into his life and daily deeds. Gradually but surely, I began to believe or feel deep down in my consciousness that one day his dreams would become reality. I began to have profound conviction about the possibility. Attracted to his conviction, generosity, and his beautiful style, I finally decided that this was the man that I had to help. I decided to marry him."

The wedding took place on a large main traditional wooden floor of the home of her maternal uncle, in Chebu-dong, Seoul, presided over by the Reverend Cho Hyang-rok. They honeymooned at Onyang Hot Springs Spa and started life together in a rented house in Daeshin-dong, Seoul.

In her 1992 autobiography, *My Love, My Country*, she recalled her marriage years:

> Fated to be a wife of a politician, I have suffered the agony of witnessing the unfair and unjust deeds inflicted upon my husband and his colleagues in their struggle for democracy. The years of pain and agony became so intense that I was unable to even cry at times. Exhausted through travail that never seemed to stop, I pleaded with God for his support and comfort....
> When we were married, my husband was an unemployed *ronin* [in feudal Japan, a samurai who lost his land and was forced to wander, often living as a bandit] because of General Park Chung-hee's coup d'etat of May 16, 1961. Marry-

ing a politician, I thought I was prepared to accept the usual ups and downs of political fortune. But I never imagined that I was destined to cross breathlessly so many painful and difficult hills and valleys of political hardship because of my husband.... Looking back, my heart still shakes uncontrollably with tears of immeasurable gratitude over the experiences of sheer miracles. So far, my husband has survived four close encounters with death ... and he again miraculously returned to life. They were unforgettable experiences, carved in my memory—a memory of resurrection of our soul and body on high-winged divine miracles.

On May 20, 1962—just nine days after marrying for the second time—Kim was arrested again, this time on charges of planning to overthrow the military government. He was detained in prison for a little more than a month before being released and found innocent of any crime.

There were a great number of South Koreans who continued to fight for democracy and human rights. Some of them created a new political party, the Min Jung Dang, in 1963; it became the second leading opposition party. Yun Po-sun, the former president under the previous parliamentary form of government, was chosen as its presidential candidate. Kim Dae-jung was selected as its spokesman. Park's followers in turn organized the Democratic Republican Party (DRP).

On October 15, 1963, a presidential election was held to determine if military rule would be ended and a civilian administration chosen. Yun Po-sun lost to Park by about 150,000 votes, though Yun contended he lost to illicit election practices.

Kim learned much from the political campaign and when parliamentary elections were scheduled later in 1963, he was nominated as the Democratic Party candidate from his home con-

Many thousands of supporters came out to Hyochang Park in Seoul in November 1970 to listen to Kim Dae-jung in his campaign for president. He narrowly lost the election, but showed enough political strength among the people to become the main opposition leader.

stituency, the Mokpo district. It was here that he was to make his mark within the opposition.

Running against five other candidates, including one with the backing of the ruling party, Kim faced an uphill fight. But then, there was a dramatic revelation. A police sergeant who supported Kim's political views made public the secret official documents that detailed the illicit measures planned to assure that ruling party candidates got elected. As a result, the minister of Home Affairs and the director of the Police Department resigned and the head of the Intelligence Section was arrested. Sergeant Ra also was arrested and prosecuted for leaking the information.

Kim won the election easily, with 22,513 votes to the runnerup's 2,615. The election raised him to a politician of national standing.

But Yun Po-sun still was the main national opposition leader. When Yun pronounced objections to plans to normalize relations with a former occupation enemy, Japan, Kim took the more moderate—and more pragmatic—road. "Many former colonies of England and France have entered into amicable relations with their former rulers," he said. "If we refuse to establish diplomatic relations with Japan, even though we are equal with Japan, we are heading against the common trend of the world. Second, we are directly facing the communists in the North. If we make Japan an adversary under such a situation, we will be facing two foes on two fronts. If we place our top priority on our national security, then such a policy would be utmost folly."

Kim Dae-jung leads a candlelight demonstration in an effort to abolish the dictatorial Yushin Constitution. The 1972 decrees, which restricted many basic freedoms, produced what many felt was the darkest era of recent Korean history.

When the war in nearby Vietnam heated up in 1965, the United States asked Korea for troops to help the fight. While Yun objected to the proposal as "selling out our blood," the moderate leaders, including Park Soon-chun and Kim, suggested sending a volunteer corps of reserve officers and soldiers. This was approved by the National Assembly.

Kim had now built up a following, both within the opposition party and among the people who sought a more democratic rule.

The new parliamentary elections in June 1967 put all that to the test.

Kim had made a strong rival, if not an enemy, of President Park when he made the disclosure of election violations in winning the National Assembly election in Mokpo four years previous. Park, it seemed, was now determined not to allow him another victory. His ruling party put Kim Byung-sam up as its candidate, with all the resources of the government at his disposal. Kim Byung-sam was a retired general who had taken part in the military coup of 1961 and later served as Minister of Communication.

The government promised new development in the Mokpo area and sent officials from the Mokpo area on paid vacations to campaign for Kim Byung-sam. Yet, with the international press watching, Kim Dae-jung was able to overcome all the obstacles and win the election. It was a major victory for him in his first major confrontation with Park.

He followed it up with an even stronger victory four years later, with a landslide parliamentary win in what many considered a direct duel with Park. The National Assembly elections were held soon after the presidential elections; Park had just won re-election as president by about one million votes, defeating Yun Po-sun, who represented the New Democratic Party, or NDP, a merger of the major opposition forces. The NDP wanted a presidential candidate for the 1971 election who was from a younger generation, "a stan-

Kim Dae-jung and his wife cast their ballots in the presidential election of 1971. Kim narrowly lost the race to Park Chung-hee, proving himself a formidable opponent.

dardbearer in his forties." Party leaders recalled a massive opposition rally in 1969, a protest against government plans to change the constitution to allow a third consecutive term to an increasingly unpopular ruling president. On that occasion, Kim Dae-jung was one of the speakers. His speech, though only fifteen minutes long, awed the crowd, which gave him a thundering round of applause. With that in mind, on September 29, 1970, at their party convention, the NDP chose Kim Dae-jung as their presidential candidate.

"A truly new era shall dawn from now on," Kim said in his acceptance speech. "A new epoch shall be marked for our party as well as for Korean politics. I shall fight for the freedom and well-being of our people as a vanguard of this new era. I shall prevent the perpetuation of the rule of Park Chung-hee at any cost and I shall bring forth a peaceful, democratic transfer of power, which has been the aspiration of our people since the foundation of our nation."

The reactions of the Park regime were harsh and dictatorial. There were well known irregular election practices, provoking Kim to say in an interview:

The press and other media for mass communication are monopolized by the government and all the power and apparatus of the administration have been actively involved in the promotion of the election. Sources of campaign funds for the opposition party have been blocked. Manipulations to split the ranks of the opposition party and suppression of opposition members have been openly carried out. I wish that the coming election will be carried out under law and order. I sincerely wish that the result of the election will reflect the wishes of the sovereign people under fair judgment. I will pledge that there will be no revenge on political grounds after the election. But if a rigged election is carried out, I shall fight standing at the head of the people and the party. I shall dedicate my own life to this cause.

As part of his presidential campaign, Kim visited the United States at its invitation. He held formal conferences with the State Department, Senator William Fulbright and Senator Edward Kennedy, who called him the "Kennedy of Korea." On the way back to Korea, he stopped to see Japanese Prime Minister Tanaka Kakuei.

Kim campaigned at home with the mottos "Repeal of the Third Term Presidency" and "Down With Dictatorship." Among the major issues in his platform were a guarantee of Korean security by the four superpowers; peaceful reunification of Korea through reconciliation and mutual exchanges between the two Koreas; promotion of a mass-participatory economy, and a wealth tax system. He attacked the corruption of the Park regime, declaring that he was "surrounded by cronies who amassed illicit fortunes amounting to tens of billions...."

On April 18, nearly one million people gathered to hear his campaign speech at Chang-Choong-Dan Park.

His pronouncements provoked dramatic responses. An explosion rocked Kim's Dongkyo-Dong residence while he was touring the United States. Thieves broke into the offices of the NDP Policy Research Department, stealing important documents. And the opposition tried smear tactics and stirred up regional animosities.

Election day was April 27, 1971. Kim received 46 percent of the vote, but lost to Park by less than one million votes.

It was, many felt, a moral victory and it made the name Kim Dae-jung known in households across the nation. When he went campaigning for opposition candidates in local elections in the weeks after the presidential vote, he invariably drew large crowds.

Despite a splint on his arm, Kim Dae-jung speaks to support National Assembly candidates at Youngdung-po in Seoul in May 1971. Kim was hurt in a car accident that appeared to be an attempt on his life.

One of those campaign trips almost cost him his life.

On May 24, 1971, Kim was on his way to Seoul to deliver a speech. He was riding in a car from the Mokpo area, since bad weather had caused the cancellation of his flight. As they drove along the highway between Mokpo and Kwangju, a taxi cut between his car, carrying Kim, his secretary and three bodyguards, and a second car, in which his younger brother and campaign aides were riding. Suddenly, they were hit in the rear by an eight-ton truck which then crushed the taxi, killing both men in it.

Kim suffered injuries to his arms, legs and hip. His secretary and one of his bodyguards had to be hospitalized.

A preponderance of evidence indicated this was no ordinary automobile accident, but an attempt on Kim's life. It was not to be the last.

5

A "Second Birthday"

Park Chung-hee's narrow victory in the presidential election of 1971 served notice that he was, to some extent, losing control of Korean society. Anti-government protests continued on many of the university campuses and there were indications, after the American withdrawal from Vietnam, and U.S. President Nixon's visit to China, that the balance of power was shifting in East Asia.

Park acted to strengthen his position and to preserve what he perceived as the stability and security of the Republic of Korea.

He declared a state of emergency in October 1972 that gave him dictatorial powers. He suspended parts of the constitution, declared martial law, and dissolved the National Assembly. He introduced a series of measures that came to be known as the Yushin (Revitalization) constitution. Included were provisions for unlimited six-year terms of office—in effect, a lifetime presidency— and decrees that anyone who objected to the new rules would be court-martialed.

Kim Dae-jung at home in Seoul. Kim was forced to spend much time there—under house arrest by South Korean government leaders.

The Yushin constitution was ratified and Park was again re-elected as president.

Kim Dae-jung was in Japan at the time; he had left for medical treatment of a hip injury just days before the Yushin measures were announced. From Tokyo, he issued a statement: "The measures promulgated by President Park Chung-hee are nothing but astonishing anti-democratic schemes to perpetuate his dictatorial rule under the pretext of promotion of reunification. These measures are outright violations of the constitution and a brutal suppression of the people's yearnings to accomplish reunification of our fatherland from the position of strength by promoting democracy in South Korea. I am confident that Park's act will be condemned by public opinion and is doomed to fail by the power of the great Korean people who overthrew the dictatorial regime of Syngman Rhee in pursuit of democratic freedom."

He continued to issue statements of protest, from Japan and from the United States, where he visited major cities and lectured to Korean residents on the political situation at home. He also met prominent U.S. foriegn policy leaders there, and got their advice and assistance, while also organizing the American chapter for the National Conference for Restoration of Democracy and Reunification in Korea.

He flew back to Japan in July 1973. It was that summer that his enemies audaciously attempted to silence him forever.

Both American CIA agents and Japanese police had received reports that the Korean CIA was following Kim in Japan and he took precautionary measures, changing hotels and registering under false names. An attempt to kill him on August 8 was thwarted by the unexpected arrival of an old political friend at his room in the Grand Palace Hotel. But it did not prevent his kidnapping.

At about 1 P.M. that day, Kim was on his way to another political meeting. As he reached the hotel elevator from his 22nd floor room, he was

Kim Dae-jung tells investigators about how he was kidnapped and nearly murdered before being let go by his captors. United States officials were instrumental in his rescue.

attacked by three men, one of whom put a chloroform-soaked rag over his face, knocking him out. They carried him to a car and drove off to a secret house in a nearby port city. Around midnight, they transferred Kim to a motorboat and took him to a bigger boat, the SS *Yong-Keum*.

His hands and feet were bound to a wooden board and two heavy stones were attached. His eyes and mouth were taped shut. He was about to be dumped into the sea and drowned.

Kim, a devout Catholic, prayed to Jesus,

"Please save my life. I still have so many things to do."

At that moment, there was a bright light and a bang. A helicopter—a U.S. military surveillance helicopter, it turned out—made a low pass over the boat. The boat speeded up and tried to evade the helicopter, which followed for a time. Some thirty minutes later, the helicopter gone, his fearful kidnappers took Kim back to land, hiding him in one place or another for four days.

On August 13, shortly before 10 P.M., the door bell rang at Kim's home, where his wife and two

Kim Dae-jung talks to reporters about his kidnapping from a Tokyo hotel in 1973. Kim had been bound and gagged and taken aboard a boat to be dumped into the sea.

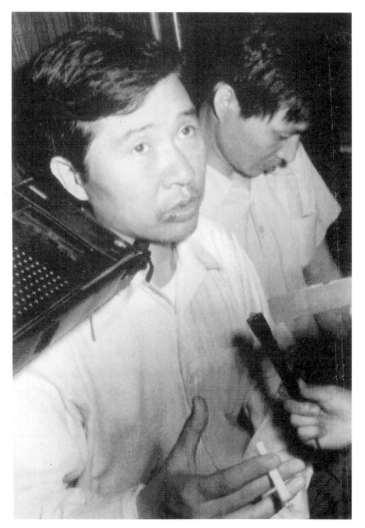

56

sons had become increasingly pessimistic and were preparing for the worst news.

Instead, it was Kim Dae-jung at the door, haggard but alive.

As his wife described it, "His lips were split and torn, his wrist where he was bound by a rope had a deep purple bruise; he had no jacket and was wearing sneakers. The kidnappers had released him in front of the Dongkyo dong Church, near the house. They said, 'After five minutes, you can take off the tape from your eyes and you can go home.' For the miraculous return of my husband, we knelt in prayer to Almighty God."

To this day, August 13 is considered his "second birthday."

Years later, it was revealed that his rescue was made possible by United States intervention.

Donald Gregg, a former CIA official and later ambassador to South Korea, later was to reveal the details of American intervention that saved Kim's life. U.S. intelligence sources had found out about the kidnapping from Japanese intelligence agents, among others. U.S. National Security Adviser Henry Kissinger and U.S. Ambassador to Japan Edwin O. Reischauer were alerted. All emphasized that Kim's life was to be saved at any cost and they must act quickly. U.S. Ambassador to South Korea Philip Habib called in key aides and said, "I know how things work here; we've got twenty-four hours to react very strongly, by saying we know who kidnapped him; and if we don't, Kim Dae-jung is dead." Habib jumped in his car and raced to the presidential Blue House to protest to the Park regime on an official basis, saying that the death of Kim would be "a stain on Korea's escutcheon."

Kim at that point was tied hand and foot on the boat in the Straits of Tsushima. A radio message was sent to the boat, just in time. Kim was taken back to land, unfettered, and eventually taken back to Seoul, where he was released a few hundred yards from his house.

In a report years later, the newspaper *Dong-A Ilbo*

> *I know how things work here; we've got twenty-four hours to react very strongly . . . and if we don't, Kim Dae-jung is dead.*
> —U.S. AMBASSADOR PHILIP HABIB

recounted the details of the abduction, citing secret government documents from the Korean CIA (now known as the Agency for National Security). It said forty-six KCIA agents were listed as having taken part in the kidnapping. Lee Chul-hee, then assistant deputy director of KCIA, was later quoted as saying that he was ordered by his boss, Lee Hu-rak, to "bring Kim Dae-jung home at whatever cost." If it weren't for the timing of the helicopter just before his abductors were ready to throw him into the sea, the cost would have been his life.

Neither the aborted assassination attempt, the kidnapping, nor the Yushin measures—which had effectively silenced dissident voices—would stop Kim Dae-jung, even though it would mean more imprisonment. He spent another year in jail in 1975 for "violation of the election law." (The government retired the original judge, who recommended leniency.)

In 1976, he demanded the nullification of the repressive decrees in his *Myong Dong Declaration for Democratization*. It called for a repeal of the emergency decrees, release of political prisoners, and freedom of press and assembly, among other demands.

As a result of his outspoken opposition, Kim was arrested on March 8, and on March 22 was sentenced to five years in the Chinju penetentiary, with a suspension of all his civil rights on charges of violating the constitution.

He told a court of appeals, futilely:

> In this country, nobody dares defy the wishes of the president of the current regime. I learned this fact through my experiences in the trial proceedings on charges for my alleged violation of the election law.... I feel sorry for the prosecutors who had to endure listening to all the defense arguments. In a country where the prosecution has no independent status and is subordinated to the man in power, they have no other choice....

Here in this court, my two sons have come to observe the court proceedings. I don't want them to feel ashamed of their father, and toward that end, I shall dedicate my entire life.
—KIM DAE-JUNG
during his statement at his trial in 1976.

[American author Ernest] Hemingway said in his *Old Man and the Sea* that man endowed with sincerity and conviction may be frustrated but will never be defeated. Our imprisoned colleagues have strengthened their faith and demonstrated more courage whenever they have been placed in great adversity and I feel that what Hemingway said has been fully vindicated....

This country has a history of growth amid challenges. I consider that we have already won a victory regardless of the verdict of the court....

Kim Dae-jung raises his hand to ask the presiding judge at his trial to allow him a final statement. Kim had been arrested on charges of violating election laws in his candidacy for president. His statement was to no avail; he was found guilty and sentenced, but later was freed.

In short, the Yushin system is not aiming for reunification, nor for national security and anti-communism, but only for perpetuation of a lifetime rule of one man. The Yushin constitution is the only means to achieve the one-man rule and is constituted toward that end. This is as obvious as the sun rises in the east. Under the present system, assurances of human rights and liberty, which are the properties of democracy, would not be feasible. Democracy and the Yushin system do not go together, as water and oil do not.

Socially, there will be no freedom of conscience, no freedom of religion and no freedom of academic institutions under the Yushin system. Under the Yushin system, there does not exist any social justice with which honest, diligent and conscientious people can succeed in their work. A system in which people dedicate their loyalty to only one man, the center, and a democratic system for all the people and for national security are not compatible. The best weapon with which to fight against communism is democracy.

He spoke optimistically of a peaceful, non-violent reunification and a free and democratic Korea in the future. He pledged to dedicate his life to that end.

During his imprisonment, Kim's wife was allowed just one visit a month. But she wrote to him often. This letter was dated August 10, 1977:

You may be able to receive this letter on your second birthday [when he was released from his kidnappers in 1973]. To send you congratulations while you are in prison may seem somewhat odd. But remembering the miraculous day you came back alive, I can only pray with thankfulness. Despite repeated humiliation, you have quietly and patiently stood up against them for so long. God will always reward you for your perseverance. I am convinced of it. Some may look at you with pity as a person who was born to a life of endless plights; you shall comprehend the deeper meaning of pain and humiliation by remembering Jesus Christ on the cross.

Let us remember that when Jesus was bearing the burdens of the cross, all his disciples abandoned him, and even Peter

Lee Hee-ho, who has been a staunch ally and supporter of her husband.

denied knowledge of Him three times. While Jesus suffered the excruciating pain of persecution, he still prayed for the forgiveness of those who crucified him. He showed us the eternity of truth and love to us all.

On too many occasions, I get teary-eyed just thinking of you and your pain from a purely human point of view. But to think of it from the point of view of religious faith and belief, I still like to think that there is a deeper hidden meaning in God's incomprehensible will. Believing that, I pray that you are able to accept the days of your pain and suffering as a period of special worth, and a truly valuable experience in your life.

I am confident that history is moving in a new direction. No one can defy God's guidance in history's inexorable march. Renew your strength through constant prayer. This time when I came to Jinju, I did not bring along Hong-gul as you asked. I wanted to take him along whenever I travel through the countryside to show him life on the farm, but the end of the summer vacation is less than a month away and he has too much to do with his school assignments. He had to stay home to get busy with his homework. Please understand the problem. I will bring him next time. We are all trying to satisfy your wishes; all of us in the family are trying to spend the time usefully by constantly exchanging views and discussing things amongst us. Do not worry about us.

I hope that you will have the will power to overcome all difficulties by always maintaining your good health. I pray that God will be with you always.

Late in 1978, Kim was transferred to a hospital room, but this, too, was in effect, a prison cell. The closed, barred windows were covered with non-transparent glass. Security agents and prison officials were in a room directly across the narrow corridor. Other agents and police were on guard nearby, inside and out.

Kim's sentence finally was suspended and on December 27, 1978, he was released from his hospital cell, bringing to an end three years of incarceration.

Upon his release, he issued this statement:

At the outset, I must offer my thanks to Our Lord for His boundless guidance and protection for the last three years. I also send the most profound and heartfelt thanks to so many of our people through-out the country and friends overseas who have supported me and my family during my imprisonment through prayers, hunger strikes, encouragement, through constant efforts to arouse public con-sciousness, and through so many other ways. I thank them for their kindness and blessings.

Despite my release from prison on pro-bation, what I grieve most is the fact that so many other political prisoners are still languishing in prison. Poet Kim Chi-ha, Professor Lee Young-duk, Reverends Yun Ban-ung, Moon Ik-hwan, Park Hyung-kyu, Koh Young-keun, Cho Hwa-jun, Kang Hee-nam, and countless other members of cler-gy, professors, journalists, students, workers, democratic persons, and many others.

I feel a deep sense of indignation at the undemocratic and narrow-minded behav-ior and actions of the government.

However, at a time when our nation's democracy is in dire peril, and when so many of our opposition members and stu-dents are in prison, my experience of a three-year imprisonment along with them

Kim Dae-jung and his wife, Lee Hee-ho, at a press conference after Kim's release from imprisonment. He served two years and nine months of an originally longer sentence that was the heaviest among those arrested for taking part in a 1976 Save-the-Nation movement.

is, indeed, a sort of personal obligation that I feel I had to discharge as well as an honor as their comrade. In that context I cannot really deny even a sense of happiness in all this personal suffering as well. Especially for me who had actively participated in the governance of this nation, and who had the great personal honor of receiving tremendous popular support in the 1971 presidential election, the three years that I spent in prison have great meaning for me.

This year began with the greatest turbulence since the national liberation, and the crisis will become even more serious with the new year. Internally, there is the problem of exploding prices and inflation. The so-called "three major scandals" have rocked the nation's conscience and morality, and the national feeling of distrust towards the government is pervasive. There is an additional sense of unease over the commencement of the American military withdrawal and the government defeat in the national election. Internationally, we can readily foresee the approach of the tidal changes that would seriously affect our nation—the peace treaty between China and Japan and the opening of diplomatic ties between the United States and China.

As my release from prison coincides with the turbulent changes, I feel a great burden of obligation to God and the country. My conviction stands unchanged, namely that the Yushin system was not established legitimately, and it possesses no rationale or justification for the happiness of our people or national welfare.

Only through the restoration of democracy in this country can we attain our national goals of freedom, justice and national unification. That is also the only way we can avoid the fate of the "Second Vietnam" and the "Second Iran." I shall always try my best to meet the expectations of our people and world public opinion.

I abhor mistaken politics, but do not hate any individual. Because of me, an unimaginable suffering and pain were inflicted on my family, my secretaries, defense counsels, relatives and friends. They were sent to prison or their lives were completely ruined. I myself had to endure

the pain, agony and humiliation of prison
life. But I continue to fight for the restoration of democracy, because I firmly believe
that my lonely and difficult struggle is the
only way we can prevent the inevitable
advent of horrible disasters not only for
the present ruling circles but for the entire
nation.

If I tell the truth, frankly, I feel pity, even
a genuine concern, for the leaders of the
present government and for their actions.

The government suffered a major defeat
in the recent national election. The government had all conceivable advantages
going for them. First, the election was held
under the frightening atmosphere of terror
and intimidation. Second, the government
had the support of a one-sided election
law, deliberately distorted to favor their
side. They had the illicit and powerful support of all government agencies and the
bureaucracy, reaching way down to the
grass roots. They spent unlimited sums of
campaign money as if money was going
out of style. In addition, a great number of
people in the democratic opposition boy-
cotted the election entirely. And yet, the
government suffered a humiliating defeat.
They may have all kinds of excuses for it,
but the defeat under the Yushin system
should indicate that its days are clearly
numbered. The Yushin system is rapidly
inviting its own political destruction. This
is the time for the government to pro-
foundly reflect on its own errors before the
solemn judgment of the people. It must
make a new start.

As its first step, the government must lift
all emergency decrees, and guarantee fun-
damental freedoms to the people. Conse-
quently, I must demand the immediate
release of all political prisoners regardless

of their original charges and so-called crimes.

Finally, I pray and hope that the new year will be a time of restored democracy, a time for healing national division, for national reconciliation and unity. I hope that the new year will become the solid foundation for the coming Eighties. Thank you.

But the hope dimmed quickly.

Kim was again placed under house arrest; it was to last another year.

The X's count the days spent under house arrest for Kim Dae-jung in 1979. This was Day 263.

6

Facing Death

The regime of Park Chung-hee was not invincible; at least Park himself was not.

On October 26, 1979, the dictator was shot to death at a dinner in Seoul by his own KCIA chief, Kim Jae-kyu, in what may have been a prelude to a coup attempt.

Martial law was imposed under the command of Chung Seung-hwa and an interim government set up with Prime Minister Choi Kyu-ha serving as acting president. The day after Choi was officially elected president on December 6, he abolished the restrictive Emergency Decree of 1975, a clampdown on political dissent, and then released Kim Dae-jung from house arrest. It was two more months, however, before Kim's civil rights were fully restored, in February 1980. There was a whiff of the air of freedom, a "Seoul Spring."

But deteriorating economic conditions and student demonstrations for more freedoms soon put

I have come to the conclusion that real well-being of the people could not be attained unless a genuine democratic political system is firmly established by ending the dictatorship which ignores the will of the people and downgrades the National Assembly.
—KIM DAE-JUNG

Kim Dae-jung wears traditional Korean dress at his home in Seoul, where he was under house arrest. Kim had just returned from two years of exile in the United States.

the nation on emergency footing once again. As the economy spiraled downward and demonstrations increased, martial law was imposed again. All political activity was banned, the National Assembly was dissolved and universities were closed. In response to the crackdown, students staged massive rallies in May 1980, in defiance of government injunctions. Among them was one that began on May 18 and was to become known as the Kwangju Incident. Some refer to it as the Kwangju Massacre.

There, in Kim Dae-jung's home district, demonstrators overran the provincial office and held it for a week. The army was sent in under the command of Generals Chun Doo-hwan and Roh Tae-woo and the violence escalated. Before it was quelled, nearly two hundred were left dead and thousands were injured. Some were to say the toll was far greater; years after the event, eyewitnesses told of bayonet rampages by paratroopers and other violences, and the debate over the number actually killed continued.

The anti-government demonstrations brought new repressions as the generals again took control. Dissident leaders were arrested—including Kim Dae-jung, who was forcibly taken from his home on May 17, accused of inciting the Kwangju demonstrations. He was also charged with belonging to pro-communist groups in the 1940s, receiving help from a North Korean spy during the 1971 presidential election, and organizing student uprisings in Seoul. He was sent once again to prison and put on trial—in a military court this time—in September 1980.

To no avail, he testified:

> In this country, evidently, there exist followers of the former president [Park] and, at the same time, there are a great number of democratic forces which pursue the principles of democracy. It is my firm belief that neither of these two groups can lead

this country by completely suppressing the other group. Our nation should adopt democracy and is capable of doing so. In order not to repeat the same misfortune again, these two groups should exchange dialogue, should debate among themselves, and should tolerate the other. This is the only way to overcome communism.

In response to the specific charges, he said:

The prosecution charged that I joined the communist camp. I was twenty years old at the time and I joined the Preparatory Committee for National Construction because its declared objective was national independence. Similarly, I joined the now defunct New Democratic Party

Military police guard Kim Daejung in court, where he was charged with treason and conspiracy in demonstrations against the ruling government in 1980. Kim was sentenced to death, but his sentence was commuted to life imprisonment. He spent years in prison before being exonerated.

71

because its alleged objective was the unification of South and North Korea. I had never been indicted before on the ground that I belonged to the leftist camp. In fact, I joined a rightist group in 1947 and, during the Korean War, I was accused as a reactionary by communists and barely escaped from execution at their hands. In spite of all this, the fabrication of charges as if I am a communist on the basis of what happened thirty-four years ago is in total contradiction with the prevailing practices of democratic countries.

The prosecution also charged that I met Chung Tae-muk, a North Korean espionage agent, during the 1971 election. However, at the time, Chung was freely going around in Mokpo City without any legal restrictions placed on him and nobody would have suspected him of being a communist....

As for the sedition charges, I feel that the charges were framed without grounds. I have never instigated anybody to stage demonstrations and I have never conspired with anybody to overthrow the government. If I were involved in the sedition conspiracy, at least there would be some evidence for the organized activities. But I never held any meeting with such an objective. When there were demonstrations by the students, none of my secretaries or associates ever participated in the demonstrations. If I conspired for sedition, wouldn't I be the one who led the demonstrations? From this fact alone, it is obvious that the indictments are all false. I issued statements appealing for restraint on May 13, 14, 15, 1980, when the demonstrations were at their peak.

Kim later said he did not even know about the demonstrations at Kwangju until July that year, when he was told about it by someone who visited him in prison.

After the staged trial, the military regime of President Chun Doo-hwan sentenced Kim Dae-jung to death, on September 13, 1980. The sentence was upheld by a rubber stamp Supreme Court the following January.

The U.S. administration of President Jimmy Carter, who had protested the human rights policy of the South Korean leaders during a trip to Seoul in 1979, now told them that the execution of Kim would have disastrous consequences to international relations. Chun delayed carrying out the sentence, awaiting the newly elected administration of Ronald Reagan, whom he expected would be more sympathetic. After Reagan's election, Washington got word that the execution was about to be carried out.

Richard Holbrooke, Carter's assistant Secretary of State for East Asian Affairs, met with Richard Allen, who was to become President Reagan's National Security Advisor. Allen was told that intelligence reports indicated that Kim would be killed before Reagan's inauguration if the incoming administration did not act quickly. Allen contacted President Chun and told him that President-elect Reagan opposed Kim's execution. Chun agreed to a sentence of life imprisonment instead and then on March 20, 1982, this was further reduced to twenty years. According to some reports, Chun agreed to commute Kim's death sentence in exchange for an invitation to be one of the first foreign leaders to visit Reagan when he took office early in 1981. Chun visited Washington and stayed at Blair House across from the White House in February 1981.

Prison had become almost a way of life for Kim Dae-jung, but his incarceration between May 1980 and December 1982 was surely the toughest time. He was in solitary confinement for the entire period, subjected to deliberate humiliation and harassment, his hair completely shaved off. He read much in Chongju Prison, from the Bible

Despite repeated humiliation, you have quietly and patiently stood up against them for so long. God will always reward you for your perseverance.
—LEE HEE-HO
Kim's second wife

⑬ 봉함엽서

서울特別市 麻浦区
東橋洞 (七八一)
李 姬 鎬

清州矯導所 內
金大中

청주시 미평동 148의
청주 0098

다음 冊을 差入해 주시오

이 사람을 보라
社會經濟史 (外文社?)
葉菜辭典 (美國出版令)
百科辭典 (最新版册)
韓国 社会 (東洋闻)
中国人과 日本人 (")
Japan as No. 1
우리 合氣圓 (")
두 도시이야기
못과 素
武士와 平和 (東京─김의진音)
老人과 바다 (" .)

1. 니여체
2. 레이몽 아롱
3. (早老)
4. ( )
5. 李萬甲
6. 傑湾屋
7. 에그라보법
8. 懷錦碩
9. 디킨스
10. 스탕달
11. 톨스토이
12. 헤밍웨이

A copy of a postcard written by Kim Dae-jung from his jail cell.

to Emmanuel Kant and Kenneth Galbraith, from Plato to Somerset Maugham, from Dostoyevsky to Charles Dickens. He became an avid gardener and devoted his lunch time and exercise period to tending the flowers, especially the azaleas.

And he wrote letters, although allowed only one letter a month to his family. He wrote his wife that four things kept him alive during that dark period: family visits, family letters, good books and tending the flowers.

In November 1980, he wrote to his wife:

Our family has gone through overwhelming ordeals since May 17 this year and they have exceeded all the past tribulations we have gone through before. The agonies and sufferings you had to bear were greater than those of any others. In spite of this, you have overcome them well. I am deeply grateful to you for your faith and courage with which you have triumphed over all these ordeals confidently and restrainedly and I am grateful to God who has bestowed such faith and strength on you. How could we have endured the last six months if it were not for the love of God and your strength? Amid these trials, I am most pleased and grateful over the fact that the faith of our family, including you and me, our children and my brothers, and our friends, have been strengthened.....

I deplore that I had not been a good husband to you and a good father to our sons by worldly standards. How much trouble have my brothers and relatives suffered because of me. My heart breaks often at the thought that so many of my friends have met with sacrifices and are destitute because of me. I can only offer my prayers invoking His blessings for them. I am happy at the thought that I have been married to such a good wife like you and I have been blessed with such decent, promising and understanding children as Hong-il, Hong-up and Hong-gul. I am fully confident about the future of my family. Once again, I beg for your understanding from the bottom of my heart, for my negligences of failing to be a good husband. Please remember to give my warmest regards to all family members.

To the wife of Hong-il, his first son (Hong-il was imprisoned at the time), he wrote:

When I told you that you should be interested in the work of your husband and help him, I did not mean to say that you should interfere with the work of your husband and dominate over him. A wife who is not associated with the work and thought of her husband is an unhappy wife, but a wife who dominates her husband, however, makes her a most miserable wife. If a wife is indifferent to the work of her husband and she is unable to render any help, she is separated spiritually from her husband. If a wife interferes with the work of her husband and dominates him, she is reducing her husband to the status of henpecked and she will be deprived of the happiness stemming from admiration of and following the lead of her husband. Therefore, the wisest wife is the one who has good knowledge and judgement regarding the work of her husband, yet she just renders her suggestions and modest advice so that her husband could make the final decision based on his own discretion.

To his second son, Hong-up, who was arrested on August 30, 1980, but released on November 11, he wrote:

Whenever I think of you, my heart is burdened with a feeling close to guilt. Simply because of the fact that you were my son, your marriage did not come through twice, even though both parties loved each other. You have been unable to find a spouse even at your present age and have been unable to land a job even though your cherished desire is to work in business. I have been no help to you, but what is still worse, I have been standing as an obstacle in your way to happiness in your married life and success in your career. It is beyond my description as to how much my heart aches to think of this situation.... I pray ... that all these painful experiences may serve you well as "fertilizer" so that they could be more valuable than gold in your future life.

Kim's wife who stood by him through his many trials, imprisonments and exiles would eventually see triumph over tragedy and oppression when she stood by him on his inauguration day.

And to Hong-gul he wrote:

I cannot describe how much consolation I have received from your letter. All my family have suffered from all kinds of hardship because of me and I cannot help but feeling heartbreak whenever I think of your ordeals. But more than anyone else, the anguishes you have undergone are extraordinary and unique. You experienced the kidnap case when you were an elementary school boy and witnessed my imprisonment when you were in the third year of middle school. For two years while you were in high school, you had come through the period of my house arrest and current trial. What unbearable shocks they must have inflicted on you during your childhood and adolescent years! I have always been feeling guilty at the thought of the sufferings which were inflicted on you against my will. Therefore, it is beyond my power of expression to describe how glad and grateful I am to see you overcome all these spiritual trials well with faith in Him and supported by His helping hands.

Kim received this letter from his wife, dated December 6, 1980:

I have received your letter today—a letter that I have waited for so long. Your letter once again reminded me of the last six months or so that I wished never existed— a period which cannot be described except with words I normally would not want to repeat. Looking back at the last half year, I can only thank God for His blessings which enabled patience and endurance. But there are still more hardships to endure and pain to suffer. I pray to God that we can continue to be patient and hopeful in the days to come.

Some may consider us to be most unfortunate people. But I would like to believe that now is the truly happy period for us all when God's blessings and grace for us have never been closer to Him; we have never communicated with Him more intimately. He will be with us always to protect us from harm's way.

To comprehend and to experience the deepest meaning of life has to be the most valuable thing in our lives. Hard and painful though it may be, all will eventually lead to your encounter with God, who is the incarnation of the way, truth, and life itself.

Because your life has not been smooth, because it has been an unending path of thorns, I love you more and respect you more. The image of you with firm faith, pleading with Jesus to overcome your ordeal is, to me, nobler than all the mundane treasures one could possess in this world. You have always extended yourself for a nobler goal—with tears and blood. You have always listened to the voices of conscience, and tried to live a life of righteousness. You have always possessed an unusually strong affection for our country and its people. The reward for all that has been your endless suffering. It has been an experience of carrying on your shoulders the bloody cross of belief and profound faith that will lead you to a true treasure of God.

When you were kidnapped, you sensed that the end was near. When you were being carried on a ship, you saw Jesus Christ standing next to you and you pleaded with him to save your life. I am convinced that a similar miracle will happen again this time. God will surely respond to your earnest pleas for help. You must always keep your faith in God intact—a faith that He will not abandon you, but will bring you new hope for tomorrow. I know it will come.

December may be the last month of the year, but to faithful believers, it is the happy month of the birth of Christ. The night is darker and it is more difficult to find one's way, a time of fear and uncertainty. Everything else seems low and depressed. But Christ has come for us as the guiding light to enable us to navigate the world of darkness. He has come to break up the night, to light our path, and to teach us new and eternal life. The deeper and darker the night, the nearer is the heralding of a new dawn. The 'night' of our life should allow us the hope of a second birth. We should, therefore, courageously shake off our disappointment, fear, and anxiety so that we can expect the peaceful light of a new morning. It is all because Jesus has shown us new things in our lives and made us have hopes and dreams. (Romans 8:15-25. "I consider that the sufferings of this present time are not worth comparing with the glory about to be revealed to us.")

I am waiting for Santa Claus to bring wonderful and happy news to our family on Christmas Day this year. I am praying very humbly that God will allow us a new day to live a life of righteousness, justice, fairness, love, and humility.

I have decided to fast and pray with Hong-up from December 8 to 10. I am hoping that our prayer will be answered. I will try to pray and please God. I am hoping that all good things will converge—a neat conclusion for us all.

Please spend your days in peace, and pray with a firm belief in the future. I am sure God is planning a new day for you—a new day for your new task. He will give you something new, not old.

On December 23, 1982, Kim's twenty-year jail term was suspended and he was transferred to Seoul National University Hospital. He was still bothered by the hip injured in the "automobile accident" in 1971 and he still walks with a limp. He also has hearing problems he said were caused when he was tortured by government agents in 1980 (he wears a hearing aid in his left ear).

The hospital proved to be a brief stop on the way to a period of freedom in the United States.

7

A Phoenix Rises

Once again, the United States showed its support of Kim Dae-jung, officially inviting him for an extended visit for a second time.

Kim was reluctant to accept, but the proposal included a pledge that some fellow prisoners would be released if he were to leave the country. Probably as important, if not more so, was his family. His wife and three sons had all suffered to some degree simply by being related to the political dissident.

His wife had stayed by his side throughout all his ordeals. "I felt as if it was my mission to assist him," she once said.

Kim had two sons by his first marriage, Hong-il, and Hong-up. On November 12, 1963, Hong-gul had been born to Lee and Kim. Hong-il, now a national legislator with his father's party, was sentenced to three years in prison in 1980, charged with helping his father. He survived through great hardship and torture. Hong-up is now a successful businessman. Kim's son from his second marriage, Hong-gul, is a doctoral stu-

> *The problem is that nature's spring comes like clockwork but life's spring has a very irregular rhythm. Sometimes it comes, sometimes it seems as if it will never come . . . Spring, however, comes as abruptly as a miracle.*
> —KIM DAE-JUNG
> From his prison cell in 1982

Kim Dae-jung walks among some of his supporters.

dent in the United States. There are seven grandchildren.

So thoughts of his family played a strong part in Kim's decision when the opportunity came to visit the United States in 1982. The family left for the United States late in December, flying to Seattle, Washington, before changing planes for Washington, D.C. In the U.S. capital, Kim was greeted by some one thousand well-wishers, including representatives from religious groups and the office of Senator Edward Kennedy, a strong supporter. At a brief airport interview with the press, he told of his gratitude to Presidents Carter and Reagan and Senator Kennedy, all of whom had helped save his life.

Kim with five of his seven grandchildren.

Kim gives a speech before the National Press Club during his visit to the United States.

The family rented a secure three-room apartment in Alexandria, Virginia, not far from Washington, and settled into political exile.

At one reception in his honor, hosted by Senator Kennedy—who had worked to help save Kim's life and bring him to the United States—Kim told the guests:

There are several grounds why the United States should be concerned with the stability and national security of Korea. The United States maintains an armed force of forty thousand men and has a big economic stake in Korea. If you support military rule, it would have only detrimental effects on such interests. The national interests of the United States would be promoted when the United States supports the aspirations of the Korean people for human rights and restoration of democracy in alliance with the people.

We do not want the intervention of the United States in our internal political

Kim is an admirable character, and one of the closing year's few examples of a victory over the sour adage "nice guys finish last." A fanatic for democracy, he was treated shamefully by the oligarchs who ran his native South Korea—that is, ran it into the ground. They jailed him, kidnapped him, tried to kill him many times. They exiled him. Through it all, he maintained his faith in popular rule and eventual vindication.
—WASHINGTON POST
1998

Kim and his wife stand with former U.S. President Jimmy Carter before giving a speech. President Carter had protested the oppression of the South Korean government and the treatment of Kim and other opposition leaders when he was President.

affairs. We do not expect the United States to intervene in our behalf to restore democracy in Korea, which is in fact our own responsibility. We want to solicit only two things from the United States: First, it should give its spiritual support to our aspiration for democracy. Second, the United States should refrain from rationalizing dictatorial regimes or from encouraging them on the pretext of guarding stability and national security. If the United States government complies with these two requests, I can assure you that we shall be able to restore democracy in Korea, which has been our cherished hope.

His sojourn in the States was filled with speeches and politicking, awards and honors, newspaper and television interviews. Emory University in Atlanta, Georgia, gave him an honorary doctor of law degree in recognition of his dedication to promoting human rights. Kim also was able to establish the Korean Institute for Human Rights, through which he hoped to strengthen his base among Korean-Americans and influence U.S. policy. The exile to the United States proved to be a busy and satisfying time. His family seemed to enjoy it as well. Hong-gul was admitted to Emory University in September 1983, and Hong-up was married in March 1984 as the Korean government finally issued an exit visa to his fiancee.

Kim also found out, after medical tests at Emory University Hospital and Georgetown Uni-

> *From a political and social viewpoint, the twentieth century might be regarded as the beginning of the masses. In order to overcome the greatest crisis in our history, that is, the division of our fatherland and the threat of communism and to attain genuine security, economic growth, and unification, the masses must be treated as the major force for change and must be treated as the master of their own destiny.*
> —KIM DAE-JUNG
> in a letter to his wife from prison
> in 1982

Lee Min-woo, president of the New Korea Democratic Party, reads a statement welcoming Kim Dae-jung on his return to Seoul in 1985. But neither Lee or any of the other Kim supporters were able to see him as government security agents rushed him through Kimpo International Airport.

Kim Dae-jung explains to American supporters how he was whisked through Kimpo International Airport in Seoul after his return from the United States and placed under house arrest. Kim hosted a dinner at his home for the Americans, including Ohio Congressman Edward Feighan (third from left).

versity Hospital that he did not need a hip operation.

But, after more than two years away from home, he was ready to return to Korea, even though he faced seventeen more years on his sentence. Senator Kennedy and other congressmen sent a joint letter to President Chun, appealing for a guarantee of safety for Kim, along with amnesty and restoration of his civil rights. At first, the government said he would have to return to prison, but through negotiations between the U.S. State Department and South Korean officials it was finally agreed that they would not imprison Kim on his return. Kim left Washington February 6, 1985.

The next time he was to set foot on U.S. soil, it would be under far grander circumstances.

Kim and his family, after a stop in Tokyo, arrived at Kimpo Airport on February 8. Whisked out of the airport through a back door, they arrived at their Dongkyo-Dong home—only to find police officers waiting there. Kim was put under house arrest again.

He was to be so confined for eighty-seven days, surrounded by hundreds of police, isolated from the outside world, not allowed visitors.

In the meantime, there were more political repressions, which led to nationwide protests and anti-government rallies in Seoul and other major cities. They became known as "grand marches for peace," their demands including a direct presidential election and repeal of the military dictatorship.

On June 29, 1985, "spring came as abruptly as a miracle," Kim was later to write of what he saw as the light at the end of a long period of darkness.

This "spring" came in the form of an eight-point declaration for eventual democratization from Roh Tae-woo, the presidential candidate of the

Plainclothes police agents block the entrance to the home of Kim Dae-jung (in background with high tree). Kim had just returned to Seoul in 1985 after two years of exile.

Kim delivers a speech during a rally attended by more than 30,000 supporters in Seoul.

Democratic Justice Party (DJP), the ruling party under President Chun. One of the concessions was for a direct presidential election. Another granted amnesty and restored civil rights to more than two thousand political dissidents—including Kim Dae-jung.

Kim now was on the way to becoming an even more formidable adversary for the ruling powers. He was one of three Kims who campaigned for the presidency in 1987—the others were Kim Young-sam and Kim Jong-pil. They lost to government candidate Roh Tae-woo, who had made a dramatic proposal. He offered to revise the constitution to allow for direct vote of the president, the first since 1971. The Kims had split the opposition vote and Roh won a five-year term with 37 percent of the popular vote.

In the National Assembly voting that followed, however, the major opposition party led by Kim Dae-jung won the largest number of delegates. Before the next presidential election, the ruling party merged with two minor opposition parties to form a new majority party that far outnumbered the supporters of Kim Dae-jung.

In 1992, the candidates were Kim Dae-jung, Kim Young-sam and Chung Ju-yung facing off in what was up until then Korea's most democratic presidential election. Kim Young-sam was elected in 1993—the nation's first civilian leader in three decades. Kim Young-sam promised to clean up political corruption; Chun Doo-hwan and Roh Tae-woo were indicted, for inappropriate use of military forces in the 1980 Kwangju uprising as well as for taking bribes from large corporations.

Kim Dae-jung started to doubt his political future. After intensive reflection, he decided it was time to leave the political arena and he headed to Great Britain to pursue new goals.

His "retirement" was not to last long, however.

Politics was in his soul—Korean politics. And so was a lifelong dedication to principles of democracy, Korean independence, and reunification. Kim Dae-jung could not sit by idly. He established

If there had not been a coup, democracy would have been established in Korea. What was wrong with having three candidates? People welcomed the three of us and they enjoyed the prevailing atmosphere of political freedom and competition. Wasn't it called a "Seoul Spring"?
—KIM DAE-JUNG
defending the 1987 presidential campaign

U.S. black leader Rev. Jesse Jackson is greeted by Kim Dae-jung during a reception in Seoul in 1986. Jackson, a supporter of Kim, was there for a three-day visit.

Kim established the Kim Dae-jung Peace Foundation for the Asian-Pacific Region to try to promote peaceful unification of the two Koreas.

the Kim Dae-jung Peace Foundation for the Asia-Pacific to promote the peaceful unification of the Koreas, democratization in Asia, and greater world peace. Inaugurated at a high-profile international conference in Seoul early in 1994, it was followed by the creation of the Forum of Democratic Leaders in the Asia-Pacific. Kim was once again in the spotlight as a symbol of democracy.

The administration of Kim Young-sam, meanwhile, was wracked by factional strife, scandal and economic crisis. Kim Dae-jung would not watch it happen from afar; he announced his return to politics on July 18, 1995. He stressed the need for a strong opposition party to counter-

balance the one-party ruling structure and founded the National Congress for New Politics. The NCNP emerged as the leading opposition party in National Assembly elections of 1996 and set the stage for Kim's triumphant presidential candidacy.

The NCNP joined forces with the minor opposition party, the United Liberal Democrats, and on December 18, 1997, after five escapes from death, one hundred and eighty-three days of house arrest, six years in prison, two exiles and sixteen years of forced retirement from politics, Kim Dae-jung was elected President of South Korea for a five-year term.

8

Let the Sunshine In

Back when U.S. President Bill Clinton was still the little-known governor of the southern state of Arkansas, Kim Dae-jung was an exiled Korean activist lobbying U.S. officials in Washington.

The two men showed how far they've come on June 9, 1998, at a White House state dinner for the new South Korean president that celebrated the triumph of democracy and U.S.-Korean ties.

In a dinner toast taking note of Kim's long years of struggle, Clinton told the South Korean president, "Through it all, you never lost hope that democracy and freedom could rise up in your native land. You remind us that at the end of all the defeats and all the trials, there is victory for the human spirit."

Kim, in turn, told Clinton that he had spent forty years under surveillance, escaped five death sentences, spent six years in prison and more than ten years in exile or under house arrest.

"Such trials signify more than my personal history," he said. "They represent the Korean people's long struggle for democracy."

God and my ancestors helped keep me alive because they have considered me a necessary political leader who has to help the people live with basic rights as human beings and to lead the country to peaceful reunification.
—KIM DAE-JUNG

President Kim Dae-jung shakes hands with outgoing President Kim Young-sam after inauguration at the National Assembly in Seoul, February 25, 1998.

U.S. President Clinton and South Korean President Kim Dae-jung shake hands during a state arrival ceremony at the White House in June 1998. President Clinton voiced confidence that, with increased U.S. trade and investment, Kim would lead a recovery of his nation's economy.

"America saved my life more than once," he added.

Towering columns of pink and white begonias welcomed White House visitors to the Grand Foyer, and the dinner menu and color scheme were strictly summer. Mauve silk tablecloths and soft lavender roses gave a warm, soft feel to the East Room, where Korean-American soprano Hei-Kyung Hong was entertaining guests after dinner.

The guest list reflected the president's request for human rights and labor leaders, with actress Margaret Cho a rare Hollywood presence. Korean-American golfer Se Ri Pak was a special request of President Kim; American Tae Kwon Do Associ-

Kim Dae-jung addresses a joint session of Congress a few months after his election as President of South Korea. Seated behind Kim is House Speaker Newt Gingrich (left) and Senator Strom Thurmond.

ation grand master Haeng Ung Lee was a special request of Clinton, as was Dean Smith, the winning former head basketball coach at the University of North Carolina.

Kim showed his regard for Clinton by doing his own Korean calligraphy on a wall hanging for the president carrying the thought: "We should respect heaven and love people." The Clintons' gifts to Kim and his wife included a Tiffany handcrafted sterling silver cache pot with an etched border inspired by a cornice found in the East Room. The dinner menu featured spotted prawns flown in from the year's first catch in Oregon, and "micro-greens" that included the tiniest sprouts that the chef could scare up.

The next day, Clinton said:

> Kim's remarkable life history reminds us that, from Seoul to its sister city San Francisco, people everywhere share the same aspirations for freedom, for peace, for the opportunity of prosperity.
>
> President Kim once wrote from his prison cell, "If winter comes, can spring be far behind?" This morning I reaffirmed to President Kim our deep confidence in his efforts to reform the Korean economy, liberalize trade and investment, strengthen the banking system and implement the IMF program. As he has said on many occasions, open markets and open democracies reinforce one another.
>
> The United States will continue our strong support for Korea's reform efforts. In this context, I reaffirmed our commitment to provide bilateral finance if needed under appropriate conditions. We also discussed a number of concrete steps to promote growth in both our countries. We explored ways to more fully open markets and to further integrate the Republic of Korea into the global economy, including

new discussions on a bilateral investment treaty. We signed an open skies agreement, which permits unrestricted air service between and beyond our countries.

I expressed my appreciation for the decision by Korean Airlines to purchase over $1 billion worth of Boeing airplanes. And I'm pleased to announce that the Overseas Private Investment Corporation has determined that Korea is again eligible for OPIC programs in response to recent steps taken to protect worker rights.

We also discussed the situation on the Korean Peninsula and reaffirmed the importance of our strong defense alliance.

President Kim Dae-jung greets International Monetary Fund Managing Director Michel Camdessus (left) and World Bank President James Wolfensohn (right) in Washington D.C. Kim told a joint session of the U.S. Congress: "What we need now, more than anything else, are foriegn investors." The IMF had granted South Korea a huge loan, but under stringent conditions.

Korea is a safer place today than it was five years ago, with a reduced nuclear threat and improved dialogue between North and South.

The United States applauds President Kim's efforts toward reconciliation. Now we hope North Korea will respond further to President Kim's gestures and that the four-party talks will make—will soon resume, because we think they also can make a crucial contribution to progress. I am pleased that yesterday, for the very first time, the United Nations Command and the North Korean military reached an agreement to hold general officer talks designed to resolve and prevent armistice-related problems along the DMZ.

On specific matters, I thank President Kim for his commitment to provide peaceful sources of energy to North Korea, and I repeated our determination to resolve problems over funding heavy fuel oil for North Korea as part of our agreement reached in 1994 to freeze its nuclear program. We will continue to provide food and humanitarian assistance, and urge our allies to do the same....

Korea has lived with the threat of war for nearly five decades. The last thing the people of Asia need now is a nuclear arms race. South Korea has set a shining example for nonproliferation by abandoning nuclear weapons, accepting safeguards in developing a peaceful nuclear program that brings benefits to the region. And the Korean people have demonstrated the universality of democratic aspirations, bringing a springtime of hope and encouragement to advocates for greater freedoms throughout Asia.

Over the last half century, America has been blessed by the presence of Korean-Americans and Korean students living and

Through it all, you never lost hope that democracy and freedom could rise up in your native land. You remind us that at the end of all the defeats and all the trials, there is victory for the human spirit.
U.S. PRESIDENT CLINTON speaking to newly-elected President of South Korea, Kim Dae-jung

learning with us. Soon, we'll be offering new work study benefits that will allow Korean students here in the United States to support themselves while in school.

Mr. President, your example reminds Americans what is very precious about our own democracy. I thank you for your visit. I thank you for your lifetime of commitment. When I go to Asia in two weeks, I will do so with a firm faith in the future of a dynamic and democratic part of the world, in no small measure because of your life and your triumphs.

Thank you.

Kim and his wife on his inauguration day as President of South Korea with all the pain of oppression behind them and the challenge of Korea's future ahead.

President Kim Dae-jung meets with IBM Chairman Louis Gerstner at the presidential house several months after his inauguration. IBM announced plans to expand its investment in South Korea with a four-point program to help in the country's export and re-engineering efforts.

Relations with the United States appeared to be the least of Kim's problems.

At home, many feared economic hardships to come under the terms of a record $57 billion bailout from the International Monetary Fund (IMF), a result of recent economic crises in Korea, the worst since the Korean War. The Korean currency, the *won*, had depreciated rapidly, raising concerns about the nation's ability to pay its foreign debts. The IMF financial help came with a price that will sorely test Kim's administration: Korea must implement austere reform programs—restraining economic growth, raising taxes and interest rates, slowing the expansion of its powerful conglomerates, the *chaebols*.

Kim had defined—and refined—his economic theories often in the past.

At the core is a strong belief in promoting the participation of all the people in all aspects of economic development, what he has termed "Mass-Participatory Economy."

"A cornerstone of my program will be to restore market functions free of government interference and to allow all groups—entrepreneurs, workers, farmers and consumers—to take full advantage of the opportunities provided by the free market," he has written.

He also opposes government intervention in economic activities, preferring a free economy in all aspects, from pricing to labor-management relations. Kim believes that politically motivated intervention in the market has produced insufficient allocation of resources, stunted the growth of small- and medium-sized enterprises, and imposed sacrifices on labor.

Kim strongly advocates an equitable distribution of wealth and opposes government "favors" to particular groups or regions. "My goal is to make sure that all people . . . participate in varying degrees in the enjoyment of the fruits of development and that no individual, group, region, or generation is forced to carry an unfairly heavy burden for the benefit of others," he has said.

On the key issue of labor-management relations, he wrote: "What is bad for the company is bad for the employees, and vice versa. Labor and management are in the same boat. Recognition of this fact is essential to realizing full participation of all groups. The government, therefore, has a moral obligation to promote harmonious and cooperative labor-management relations by playing a constructive role as an impartial but interested arbitrator."

Barely months after he took office, Kim was tested on labor-management controversy when thousands of workers went on strike to protest layoffs. Kim's administration repeatedly promised to do its best to minimize job losses—an expected

> *Never have Korea's institutions—the military, labor, business, students—been so weak. This is a challenge, but it is an opportunity as well.*
> KIM JONG HWI
> former national security adviser

effect of the IMF bailout—but promised stern punishment for illegal strikes, urging workers to talk rather than walk out and possibly scare off foreign investment, essential to reviving the Korean economy. The nationwide strike soon weakened, with the dominant twenty-six thousand unionized workers of Hyundai Motors Company returning to work just days after the strike started, choosing to negotiate with management.

Kim is optimistic for his country's future. He has said that Korea will make full economic recovery and by the year 2015 will be among the top five economic powers in the world.

In foreign relations, Kim must deal with the long-lasting problem of reunification with the North. Over the years, he has advocated a more flexible approach toward North Korea, with expanded contact and dialogue while offering aid to his impoverished communist neighbor. His policy of openness toward the North is being called *Sunshine.*

His three principles: (1) gradual and peaceful integration and unification of the two Koreas through mutual recognition; (2) efforts are necessary to safeguard stability to ensure deterrence of potential North Korean provocations; and (3) a Sunshine Policy to gently lead the North toward reforms.

In his inaugural acceptance speech, his first address to his nation as president, Kim noted the tasks ahead and set the agenda for the 21st century in Korea:

On Politics:

> We will establish a "participatory democracy"—a government in which the people are the masters and wherein the people participate together in the governance of the country. I will begin a direct dialogue with the people more than twice a year through the medium of television....

He'll want to show past Korean leaders that you don't need totalitarian rule to expand economic growth. Mr. Kim understands the problems we face, he has the right set of solutions and if he sticks to them, we will be able to overcome this crisis.
KIM JONG IN
economist

On Economics:

I will faithfully implement the agreement with the IMF. Painful as it may be, it is the road that we must take. Reform without pain is not possible. We will use the opportunity for implementing reforms so as to reinvigorate our economy. We will show the world that the Miracle on the Han River is not finished at all. We shall practice the market economy—fully and thoroughly; and we shall open our market without hesitation. We will create a new environment for foreign investors to invest in Korea without fear or reservation—a paradise for business.

In the 21st century, inducing foreign investment will be even more important than mere trade. The government will do its part in inviting foreign investment and will make sure that they will be treated the same as our own people....

On Society:

The greatest welfare for the people is to provide jobs for those who want to work. We shall provide the aged with opportunities for work and to train the handicapped. We shall not allow people to be depressed by making them feel that they are being abandoned through inaction and the lack of programs. The new government will place a high priority on the solution of the unemployment problem.

The 21st century is a century of economy as well as culture. Our culture is the national power. We shall promote our culture and the arts, but shall not interfere with them; we shall promote the culture industry as the backbone of our future economy.

On National Security:

> To strengthen our national security, we will preserve and maintain our alliance ties and close cooperation with the United States—the central factor to our national security.
>
> For peace and stability in the Korean Peninsula, we will do our best to elicit positive cooperation with the four major powers around us—the United States, Japan, China and Russia. Since I was a presidential candidate in 1971, I have advocated consistently the Four Power guarantees for Korean peace. The need for it has increased today....
>
> Through direct dialogue with the North, we shall search for a way to settle our problems between our two separate peoples. To do this, the implementations of the "Basic Agreement" between the two Koreas signed in 1991 is most crucial. The Basic Agreement is an international agreement that the two sides ought to observe. I, therefore, propose to North Korea a resumption of the inter-Korean dialogue on the basis of that agreement.

On International Relations:

> We shall faithfully abide by all the agreements and commitments we made to the other nations. Including our economic difficulties, our national reality is serious. We need positive cooperation and assistance from the world. To deserve this, we will exert our best effort to promote friendly and cooperative relations with all the nations.

And then an appeal to the people:

Lastly, I would make an appeal to the people of Korea. Please give me your help. Without your help, nothing can be done. With your help, I will not fail you or disappoint you.

I have prepared myself for a long time for the job that I am about to undertake, and I am confident that I will do the best job that I am capable of doing....

Kim Dae-jung, here as president-elect, is jubilant after speaking to the National Assembly the day after his election as President of South Korea. His victory came after years of persecution, imprisonment, house arrest and several attempts on his life.

Further Reading

In the Name of Justice and Peace. The New Democratic Party. Seoul, Korea, 1991.

"Building Peace & Democracy: Kim Dae-jung Philosophy & Dialogues." *Korean Independent Monitor*, New York, 1987.

Dae-jung, Kim. *Prison Writings.* University of California Press. Berkeley and Los Angeles, California, 1987.

Byong-kuk, Kim. *Kim Dae-jung: Hero of the Masses, Conscience in Action.* Ilweolseogak Publishing, Seoul, Korea, 1992.

Hee-ho, Lee. *My Love, My Country.* Center for Multiethnic and Transnational Studies, University of Southern California, Los Angeles, California, 1997.

Aquino, Corazon; Arias, Oscar; Dae-jung, Kim, eds. *Democracy in Asia.* Asia-Pacific Peace Press, Seoul, Korea, 1995.

Hart-Landsberg, Martin. "Korea: Division, Reunification & U.S. Foreign Policy." *Monthly Review Press*, New York, 1998.

Chronology

Dec. 3, 1925	Born on Ha-ui Island
Dec. 1943	Graduates from Mokpo Commercial High School
April 9, 1946	Marries Cha Yong-ae
June 1954	Runs in parliamentary elections in Mokpo district
May 29,1960	Cha Yong-ae dies
May 14, 1961	Elected to the Fifth National Assembly (dissolved four days later after amilitarycoupe by Park Chung-hee)
May 10, 1962	Marries Lee Hee-ho
Nov. 1963	Elected to Sixth National Assembly
June 1965	Named spokesman, Minjungdang (People's Party)
1967	Completes non-degree graduate program at the Institute of IndustrialManagement at Kyunghee University, Seoul
1970	Earns Master's Degree in Economics at Kyunghee University
April 27, 1971	Wins 46 percent of the electoral vote in presidential election, barelylosing to Park Chung-hee
May 24, 1971	Injured in automobile accident in suspected assassination attempt
Oct. 1972	In self-imposed exile in Tokyo after Korean constitution suspended by Park
Aug. 13, 1973	Released by abductors after being kidnapped in a Tokyo hotel and nearly drowned by Korean CIA agents
March 1976	Arrested on charge of violating Yushin Constitution and sentenced to five years in jail
Dec. 27, 1978	Sentence suspended; placed under house arrest
Dec. 1979	Granted amnesty after assassination of Park
1980	Forcibly arrested on May 17 by Martial Law Command; charged withtreason and sentenced to death Sept. 13
Jan. 23, 1981	Death sentence upheld, but commuted to life imprisonment by Chun
March 20, 1982	Sentence reduced to 20 years
Dec. 23, 1982	Prison term suspended; allowed to go to the United States for medical treatment
Feb. 8, 1985	Returns to South Korea; placed under house arrest
June 29, 1987	Cleared of all outstanding charges; full rights restored
Nov. 12, 1987	Founded and elected president of Party for Peace Democracy
Dec. 16, 1987	Receives 27 percent of electoral vote in first direct presidential election
April 9, 1991	Founded New Democratic Party; elected its president
Sept. 16, 1991	Founded Democratic Party (in merger with old Democratic Party)
Dec. 1992	Gets 34 percent of electoral vote in presidential election; leaves South Korea and retires to Great Britain
July 1995	Returns to politics in South Korea
Sept. 5, 1995	Founded National Congress for New Politics (NCNP)
Dec. 18, 1997	Elected President of the Republic of Korea
Feb. 25, 1998	Inaugurated as President

Index

Norm Goldstein is a writer and editor who has authored a number of biographies, including those of John Wayne and Frank Sinatra, as well as a history of the U.S. Marshals. He received a B.A. from Brooklyn College and an M.A. from Pennsylvania State University. He lives and works in New York.

Arthur M. Schlesinger, jr., taught history at Harvard for many years and is currently Albert Schweitzer Professor of the Humanities at City University of New York. He is the author of numerous highly praised works in American history and has twice been awarded the Pulitzer Prize. He served in the White House as special assistant to Presidents Kennedy and Johnson.

Photo Credits:
AP/World Wide Photos: pp. 2, 12, 14, 16, 21, 25, 47, 52, 55, 56, 59, 64, 68, 87, 88, 89, 90, 91, 94, 96, 97, 99, 102, 107; U.S.Army photo: p. 32

jB
KIM

Goldstein, Norm

Kim Dae-jung

$19.95

DATE			